GROW
WITH YOUR
FAILURES

GROW
WITH YOUR
FAILURES

GROW THROUGH YOUR FAILURES

BY

KURT GASSNER

My-mindguide.com

Grow with your failures
Kurt Gassner

All rights reserved
First Edition, 2022
© Kurt Gassner, 2022

It is unlawful to reproduce, copy, or distribute any portion of this study using electronic methods or otherwise. The reproduction of these materials is disallowed, with the exception of written distributor authorization. All resources are retained.

This statement of principles is approved and endorsed by the American Bar Association Committee and the Publications and Associations Commission.

The statistics herein are solely for instructional purposes, and the details cannot be explicitly guaranteed.

The markings used shall be without permission, and without the approval or the help of the proprietors. All logos and trademarks in this book are for information purposes only and are held explicitly by individuals who are not affiliated with this document.

Impressum
My-mindguide – The publishing trademarke of trendguide Capital GmbH, Klenzestr. 42a, 80469 Munich, Germany.

Reg. Nr. HRB Munich 206639, VAT 152 123 159, CEO: Kurt Friedrich Gassner
Web: www.my-mindguide.com, mail: gassner@my-mindguide.com

Paperback ISBN: 978-3-98793-998-3
Ebook ISBN: 978-3-949978-44-9
Hardback ISBN: 978-3-949978-43-2

TABLE OF CONTENTS

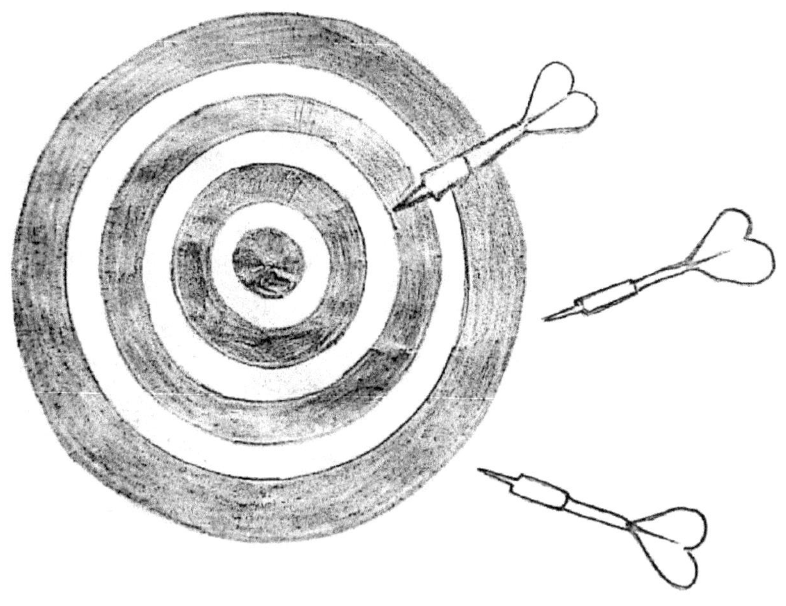

My-mindguide.com

INTRODUCTION

What is failure to you?

To many people, the above title question seems rather odd. The next logical reaction from such people would be "how on earth could I ask how one perceives failure when right from our earliest school days, we were taught to abhor failure? We heard it from teachers, parents, friends, friends' parents, and so on and so forth.

Some of such statements were probably as follows:
- "You cannot afford to fail."
- " If you fail in school, you cannot get a good job!"
- "Anyone who fails cannot amount to anything good in life."

As we passed from grade school to high school to college, we kept hearing the same talk about failure over and over again that we made conscious efforts to pass our exams in flying colors.

Failure was never an option. Any of our colleagues who was unfortunate to fail was labeled a no good and was taunted in front of the class and told that he or she would never amount to anything in life.

Unfortunately, the emotional and psychological effect of such statements made some of those people taunted and intimidated accept what was told them as the truth and they just wandered through life without any achievement.

However, very few of us, who never accepted such statements, tried everything possible to prove our worth and we won.

I am here to tell you now that you can win too.

Why am I writing this book?
All my life, I've been met with failure over and over again. This has taught me that failures are simply stepping stones to success, and every loss has brought lessons that I will share with you in this book.

The giant red F at the top of the page of homework, or a test. Even if you went through school with a 4.0, you probably have had nightmares about how soul-crushing it would be to get one, because of what it stood for: failure. Of course, the insidious thing about failure is it causes another F - fear. Fear is like a decease, crippling and devastating if allowed to run rampant in the human frame. So, to avoid fear, we should do everything we can to avoid failure, right?

Wrong. I think we need to embrace failure—Failure's ok, and I'll tell you why.

By the end of this book, Your view on failures will change, and you will learn how to channel the result of every failure to achieve your goals and aspirations.

1

There is no Real Success Without Knowing Failure

YEs, I know; it's a pretty bold statement to declare that you can't experience success without knowing failure, but it is something that I personally know to be true. I say that with conviction because it is one of those lessons that will, at some point, come into your life. What you do with that failure experience can contribute to your success or, Heaven forbid, totally deplete you of confidence and create a life with a never-ending progression of disappointments if you allow that to happen.

Failure is something that everyone I know has faced in some way, and at some time. It may be in a relationship went wrong, a job or business that went bust, or simply not reaching a goal such as losing weight or finishing a course. No one gets away in this life without going through, and feeling the anguish of failing. But if you truly believe in yourself, failure is not a shameful badge to wear; it is just a stepping stone to success, and a very powerful stepping stone.

I have certainly had failures in my life, maybe more so than many people because I am a big risk taker. I am the kind of person who thinks and believes that I can do anything. That is a bit of a double-edged sword. It is good thing because I am open to experiment a variety of experiences and jobs and relationships, and that means gaining experience and learning lessons. It is troublesome because it means I can't do everything that I think I can, so I spend a lot of time spinning my wheels on things that aren't important, and yes, failing sometimes. To add to that, I don't give up efficiently, but I consider that to be strength as opposed to a weakness. I have learned to take failure into stride, but it wasn't always easy.

When you are undergoing some kind of failure in your life, you may feel incredulous that this could ever happen to you. I look at that reaction as not being aware of who you are, and where your capabilities lie, and recognizing that even you have some limits. If you have taken on a job that is way beyond your experience and you think you can handle it that is where trouble and lessons in life come into play. Failures can teach you and provide invaluable insight if you take the time to assess "the why and the where" you went wrong. Although it is good to reach for the stars when you have a goal, you better have the right medium to get you there. Failures mean gaining experience and alerting you to the fact that something important was missed along the way. So you need to understand what that is and why, and take that knowledge to create a better experience. When you apply what you learn from your mistakes and failures, that is what creates your foundation as a human being. It builds strength, character and infinite awareness. Those are the gifts of failure.

I started my journey quite early as a young man when I founded GBK+ Partner. I was 20 years old and that gave me the much-needed business knowledge as I led the advertising agency with other business partners (My Team).

Due to the fact that I was the only bread winner and the other partners were not pulling their weight, the business inevitably shut down. That made me sad but I had to move as failure wasn't the end of me.

So my failures have led me to where I am today, and that is in an excellent place. I learned a lot of things about myself with each failure. Every failure brought a gift wrapped lesson to me and, when I looked inside and applied the knowledge from those lessons to my next venture, my success began to rise. I became more aware and focused. Failures built up my character and perseverance and strengthened my will and resolve to always do better. It made me clearly aware of some of my flaws but, more importantly, it highlighted my strengths.

We are human. We are fallible and we make mistakes and undergo some failures. That doesn't work mean that you personally are a failure, it simply means that you haven't navigated through all the stepping stones to the specific success victory that is intended exclusively for you. So, don't fear failure, because it can lead you straight to your success.

Each one of us wants to live more fulfilling and happy life: Most often, we read many articles, books and quotes explaining the recipe to become successful. Although the words incorporated in them are so motivating most of the times, they fail in making any impact on our lives. Moreover, why it is so? The answer to this question is another question. Yes, do we observe the depth of the words? No, what we do is we just scan another bunch of words seeking for success.

One such quote I came across says, "If you want to succeed in life, form the habit of doing things that failures don't like to do. We cannot judge any person by merely looking at him. However, daily, we come across three types of people in our life. The one who are satisfied and famous, second who are unsatisfied and deprived and the third, who try to do something new every day, fails in achieving it by end of the day and then make a try again in a different way. What will you rate these three type of persons? Let me guess, the first one is a successful person and other two are failures. Here it is where we make a big mistake.

People who are preserving their possessions by the fear of losing it and showing that they are thoroughly satisfied and enjoying life are failure.

In addition, the persons who see the past, have excuses and wishes but do not have guts to make it happen are the failures.

Here is where we find the answer to the quote above. The only thing, which failures do not like to do, is to make a TRY. Trials play the flip part of the coin, the coin of life. Trials may be tragedy or triumphs, but one good thing you can assure about it is, you will learn something from it—if it works, be happy and keep going with your experience because triumphs don't come without efforts; and if it don't then stop yourself from repeating the same mistake, try to analyze where you're going wrong.

Most successful people have never searched for success actually, in fact, they are the busiest people around us because they just did things, which they loved to do and believed that they can do, and in doing so, they made many mistakes and came across many failures. However, the only different thing they did from others was, they tried to learn from their mistakes and avoided repeating it. That is the best quality of a successful person.

If you want to be successful, you need to learn how to turn your negatives into positive.

Your failures are the opportunity to begin again. You may find many obstacles that will set you back and disappoint you but, you need to overcome it and move on.

You need to keep your eye on what you want and not the other way round. Failures are just the events and never a person, until he quits or give up, you need to persist your aim until you have satisfaction of doing your job well and you attain your ultimate objective.

Lesson

Every time you fail, you get another opportunity to succeed. Let failure be your motivation, and success will be inevitable.

I CAN DO IT

My-mindguide.com

2

Fear of Failure

Dealing with fear of failure is the modern-day bubonic plague, contaminating millions upon millions of people. Many people struggle from a fear of failure, even if they do not recognize it or admit it. I am certain that millions and millions of people forsake dreams for relationships, careers or hobbies because of fear of failing.

Unfortunately for most of us, our brains were programed to believe that failure is bad. Look at our education system - get good grades you get praise, bad grades and you get a big F, and likely some form of punishment. No wonder we have a hard time stepping out of our comfort zones!

One of the biggest obstacles to overcome on our road to success is the fear of failure. For some people, fear motivates them to tackle their obstacles head-on. But for most people, the fear of failure stops them in their tracks. Sound familiar? Of course it does, we've all experienced it. We have all experienced fear, we have all been afraid to do certain things. But we can change that; we can overcome this fear of failure. How? Well, for one thing we must de-condition our belief that failure is bad. Failure is not bad, it's how we learn. It's, not the only way we learn, but it is effective.

It is not failure itself that we fear it's what we believe about failure that scares us. We may believe failure will lead to rejection, looking stupid, being laughed at, ridiculed, pushed away. But how often does any of that really happen? Not very often, does it?

If you went to school, then you have almost certainly been trained to fear failure from an early age. Here's why: Getting, the "right" answer the first time, is the only thing that is rewarded in most schools. Getting the wrong answer is punished in a variety of ways: low grades, scolding and contempt from teachers and peers.

Failing is certainly not seen as a prerequisite for success. But is "getting it right the first time" really the way entrepreneurs succeed in the real world? Not at all.

When it comes to starting a business, any successful person will tell you that the fastest way to succeed is to jump in, make things happen, and be OK with failing repeatedly. "Fail fast and fail often" is a saying you've probably heard in entrepreneurial circles.

However, in school, were you taught to jump in and make things happen, even if that meant you didn't get it right the first time? Were you rewarded for not being afraid to fail? Probably not (unless you were extremely lucky). Most schoolchildren learn early that if they fail, they get a big, red F on their paper — and all the unpleasantness that goes along with that.

This means that, by the age of 18, you've been very effectively trained to fear failure. You've certainly not been trained to embrace failure as a key step in learning.

If you went to school for 12 years, this means that you've basically been "in training" to fear failure not for one year, not for two, but for 12 years straight. (If you went on to college, we can extend that to 16 years or more.)

Many psychologists have recognized that the underlying cause of fear of failure is actually fear of the resulting shame or embarrassment. The actual incident, such as flunking a college course, is not the real problem, it is the accompanying emotion of unworthiness that it provokes. People want to avoid this painful experience, so they self-sabotage or behave in self-protective ways, such as not taking risks.

Trying and failing would confirm what they already fear — that they are not smart enough, talented enough, lovable enough, etc. The fear of confirming that unworthiness is stronger than the despair they feel at giving up their dream. This shows the power of shame.

My second business taught me another great lesson to never let anyone interfere with how you run your business. For me, it was my wife.

I created a catalog as well as a video and sold it. I really made much money on the advertising materials, so I decided to go into the lingerie business. My wife thought the plan was not solid enough and didn't want to be involved, so she discouraged me. I sold the company five years later.

It's amazing how we are sometimes controlled by others—not only physically, but emotionally.

What is the one thing you have always wanted to do and never did because of people's opinions or disparaging remarks?

When we are young, we have our parents to tell us what is right or wrong, or tell us what we must or must not do. Well, we are beyond that, now. We are grown ups and should be able to decide what we want to do with our lives. That's all well and good, but as we get older, we are afraid to make a change and, sometimes, we ask others for their advice. We think it is a method of security to ask others if we should do something or not, but it can be discouraging and a real downer.

The most painful thing is, though I made much money in the business, the company I sold it to makes much more, well into millions. I made a wrong business decision because it didn't sit well with my wife, which brings me to my next point…

Fear can interfere (or should that be "inter-fear"?) with our progress as leaders, as business owners, as goal achievers. We all possess some level of fear, so the good news is, we're not in it alone! The better news is, when you learn to exercise control over your fear, you learn to exercise one of your greatest powers – the power to choose!

Let's have a chat about fear... essentially fear can be broken down into three basic categories: fear of failure, fear of criticism or rejection, and fear of the unknown. Although any one of these can cause you to become immobile, it is usually a combination of all three that creates the most difficulty. A closer look at the characteristics of these fears will reveal them for what they really are – imaginary obstacles to our success.

It is all too common for people to really want something but never even try to go after it. Why? We can chalk that up to the fear of failure. If we recognize that, by not trying, failure is certain, the comicality of this thought would become clear. Unfortunately, this notion of not going for the things we want is a regular occurrence for many of us. Why? We tends to lose perspective of what it means to fail. With failure comes the opportunity to learn and grow. In other words, to fail is to learn. The point is, without failure there is no progress. When you stop falling (or falling), you stop learning. Failure is important to success when you view it as an opportunity to learn.

Fear of Criticism

Let's say Lucy, a salesperson, asks for an order and doesn't receive it; all that means is that she simply didn't get the order. Every time this happens, Lucy often views the transaction differently and concludes that she, not the product, was rejected. Lucy then beings to convince herself that she's not as good a salesperson as her colleagues and that she is probably not worthy of the order. She then stops asking for orders rather than risk the chance of rejection. At this point, Lucy, and any salesperson in this situation, should pause and put things into perspective. She needs to realize that her worth as an individual is not on the line, only the sales order at hand.

Fear of the Unknown

Many times, our need for security (the need to feel safe), causes us to be fearful in those situations where we're not sure what is going to happen. Our fear of what might or might not happen can cause us to keep from doing those things that will MAKE happen what we want to happen.

Conquer the Fear

Each of the fears mentioned earlier can hinder success, growth and goal achievement, so it's important to remember that every one of us possesses fear to some extent. Fear is inhibiting only when it is allowed to control your life to the degree it causes inactivity and indecision. When you exercise control over your fear, you exercise one of your greatest powers...the power to choose!

Fears are thoughts. Because you have the power to exercise complete control over your mind, you can replace fearful thinking with positive ideas, realistic expectations, and a new attitude about "learning experiences.

How to Overcome Fear of Failure

Past experiences often shape what our fears will be in the future. We must not let our fears paralyze us and leave us in fear. We should let it be a learning experience and become even better. We must realize that many people who are successful today have experienced failure at some point in time. If it was not for that failure, some of them would not even be where they are at today. We must take failure and use it to our advantage instead of letting it discourages you allow it to give you that extra boost and drive to do better.

The next leading cause to this is lack of confidence – this alone can destroy you. People who are confident have no fear of failure because, in their mind, they know there are going to succeed no matter what even if they do run across some bumps in the road. Confident people will not let any bumps in the road stop them from there success because, most of the time, people who are confident have a more positive outlook on life. They will not let anything come in the way or distract them from their goal. They do not worry about and/or allow circumstances or other people stop them from reaching their goal. Which brings me to the next subject which is comparing our self to other people and worrying about what they think.

We must not worry or compare our self to other people. That is doing nothing but putting unnecessary stress on our self. We often worry about living up to other people's standards instead of trying to live up to our standards. We should create are own meaning of success rather than trying to live up to somebody else's purpose of success. It really should not matter what other people may think or say about you and how you feel about success. People are going to think and say what they want all that really matters is if you are happy and/or pleased with what you are doing. Make you own path and standards for what best pleases you regardless of what others may think, feel or say about it.

Are You Saying No to Who You Are Meant to Be?
We all know that Thomas Edison invented the light bulb.

Did you know he also invented the stock ticker, the electric vote recorder, the automatic telegraph, the electric safety miner's lamp, fluorescent lights, the motion picture camera, and the phonograph?

While struggling with the light bulb, he replied, "I have not failed seven hundred times. I have not failed once. I have succeeded in proving that those seven hundred ways will not work. When I have eliminated the ways that will not work, I will find the way that will work." From the book, "The Power of Patience," by M.J. Ryan.

- Do you have a fear of failure?
- Do you cringe at the thought of making a mistake?
- Do you expect the worst to happen rather than the best?

Fear of failure is a common reason people hesitate to say YES. For many, the attachment to doing something that leads to an expected or desired outcome often determines whether an experience is viewed as positive or negative. It's only good if it goes the way you want.

If you do something that does not lead to the outcome you desire or hope, how do you use that experience to help you positively? Do you see it as a learning opportunity or a reason to beat yourself up?

Being successful in any area of your life includes a learning curve. That means making mistakes and experimenting with decisions and actions to create the life you are here to live. Accomplishments can be defined as the completion of an action. ANY action. I encourage you to be willing to recognize and appreciate your courage to both succeed and fail—which is all a success, really!

How about Oprah? If you look at where, she started. Whom she has become, her rise to becoming a powerful influence for women has soared over the years because she has had the guts to set a new standard for talk shows and the willingness to be a transparent model of authenticity to people worldwide.

How about you? Are you the same person you were five years ago? If you've been growing yourself and your business, the answer would be no. Even if you haven't put a lot of time and energy into personal growth, it is impossible to remain the same indefinitely. We are either moving forwards or we are moving backward.

We use past experiences as a barometer to measure future experiences and projected outcomes. We can hesitate to say YES because we believe, "If this happened in the past, I fear the same experience will repeat in my future." We can use past experiences as excuses to take risks and take quantum leaps. To expect the past to repeat itself exactly is impossible because we aren't the same people today that we were then. The potential for themes and patterns to recur is probable if you haven't done the inner work to clear limiting beliefs, resolve past pain, and self-sabotage.

We can manufacture any reason to avoid doing anything we don't want to do. The more evidence we collect to prove our reasoning, the better positioned we are to make our case to ourselves and to others. And we can become brilliant in our defense to avoid stepping out of our comfort zones or retreating when the going gets tough. Enlisting others to support our case makes things a whole lot easier to avoid.

Common beliefs regarding failure:
- I have to get it right (perfect)
- I don't have what it takes
- If I say no, people won't like me
- I have nothing valuable to offer
- If I'm really "me" people won't like or love me
- Things don't usually turn out well for me (self-fulfilling prophecy?)
- It's too hard
- Success happens for other people not me
- I'm not good enough, smart enough, lovable enough...
- I'm not ready
- I won't be able to handle...
- Maybe what I have is enough and I should be happy with the way things are and not want more.

Self-fulfilling prophecies give us even more ammunition to prove why something doesn't work out well. Wikipedia's definition of self-fulfilling prophecy is "a prediction that directly or indirectly causes itself to be true." If we are resistant, expecting something to go poorly or fear it might go well (fear of success), you can bet we'll find ways to sabotage ourselves so we can prove we're right. That gives us permission to come back and say, "I told you so!" to ourselves and others because we didn't really say YES!

It is through the trial and error experiences that we develop our unique formula for happiness and success.

Yes, you will minimize the chances of too many costly mistakes in your life by doing your homework, making informed decisions, and creating solid strategies to implement. Remember, that even with the best plan that includes anticipating possible outcomes; life will still bring you the unexpected. When you have failures and mistakes as part of your strategy to success and outlook on life you will rebound more quickly to each situation as it arises. Hence, that you continue to move toward your destination.

Getting things you may not want will help you get that much clearer about what you do want. In that way, your commitment to your dreams and goals become more compelling.

To explore your attitudes about failure, consider the following twelve questions. Take your time in answering them:

- What is your definition of failure?
- What does failure mean to you? What does it look like, feel like?
- What fears, concerns, or assumptions do you associate with failure?
- How are your fears and beliefs about failures affecting your life? Constricting you? Inspiring and motivating you? Some people use their fear to break through barriers and create amazing lives.

- Is it possible that your fears and beliefs about failure are fundamentally false, even if you have evidence to back it up?
- If you fail at something, does that define you as a failure?
- What specific experiences would you define as failures?
- Can there be success in failure? (Remember Thomas Edison's quote!) Is it possible that any every failure you ever had was really a success?
- Do you use your past failures as learning experiences or do you use them to beat yourself up?
- If you appreciate past failures as growth and healing opportunities, what value have you have taken from them to enhance your life?
- If you could not fail, what would you be doing? Whom would you be?
- Would be saying YES to whom you are meant to be?

We are human beings! We react, respond, screw up, and do things brilliantly.

Every situation offers a growth and healing opportunity. Look for the gifts and blessings in each experience that challenges you and invites you to be more than you are, especially when it is undesired.

- Approach life with more self-love and compassion for those times you judge yourself to be less than your best.

- Aspire to see yourself and others through the eyes of love (if you aren't already there!). And when you have those moments when you slip into your humanity rather than your Divinity, forgive yourself and use the experience as an opportunity to heal and grow.

- Don't take yourself so seriously. Remember to laugh and have fun.

Fear of success and fear of failure are two sides of the same experience. By definition, success and failure is perceived from multiple viewpoints. Both results offer opportunities for self-discovery and change. It is through the process of succeeding and failing that we come to know more about who we are. We learn about our unique talents, skills, and gifts through the opportunities we create that invite us to shine.

Lesson

***Don't let fear keep you from taking risks. If you succeed, you're wise…if you fail, you'll learn.
Don't forget that***

FAILURE
SUCCESS

My-mindguide.com

3

The Western World's Perception Of Failure

One of the defining differences between entrepreneurial cultures in the United States and Europe is their respective approach to "failure." These approaches can literally seem like day and night. The U.S. is well known for its tolerance of entrepreneurial failures, where the emphasis, correctly (as with anything in life), is always: Try again, try harder, and the only real loser is the fighter who remains down for the count. Indeed, the mantra in Silicon Valley has become "fail often, fail fast" (though there are many objections to this oversimplification), the governing principle being that the more mistakes are made earlier on, the faster entrepreneurs learn and the better their business models become for future attempts.

In Europe, by contrast, entrepreneurism has historically been discouraged precisely on the basis that it will possibly end in failure, failure is shameful, and therefore that employment with established businesses is worthy of far more respect. This attitude has permeated European attitudes for generations, buttressed by varying social democratic models emphasizing social security over free enterprise, a necessary corrective to forms of capitalism in which not everyone can compete on the same level, but which has also had the effect of erecting far more bureaucratic barriers to free enterprise and regulations than in the U.S. One consequence of this has been that Europe's startup scene is materializing markedly slower by comparison, its ecosystem is deeply fragmented, and its products are often derivative of American innovation. Why bother to compete? Then, say some. For European entrepreneurs, staring across the pond longingly at a bustling Silicon Valley can often feel like a lonely experience.

In Europe, then, failure is perceived as a negative, hushed up, whispered about and hidden like the crazy old uncle in the attic. But Europeans may not have the luxury of this perception much longer. Employment rates remain lethargic, with close to 10% out of work and unemployment hovering close to the 20 million mark in the EU-28. Some of the reasons for this is structural, such as the traditional economy being overhauled by new forms of technology, requiring constant re-training, and the broader disappearance of jobs since the economic crisis. But it also means that with less opportunity, more individuals across generations who are looking for work are being compelled to consider the option of setting up their own businesses: by definition, this means more people will be forced to adopt an entrepreneurial mindset. Growing pains aside, this could have the benefits of loosening restrictions on business, something the European Commission is actively pursuing, and fostering greater inter-generational cooperation and between sectors. But what does this mean for the culture of failure in Europe?

There are some signs that European attitudes may be changing, starting with the noticeable uptick in start-up activity in recent years, some moderate demonstrable successes, and, with necessity being the mother of invention, an emerging mindset among individuals that taking a risk and failing may be preferable to the biggest risk of all: doing nothing. In this light, negativity has more to do with the remaining, often unpredictable and seemingly insurmountable challenges ahead, than with the idea of entrepreneurship itself. And severe cultural challenges do remain: individuals may hesitate because they fear picking the wrong career path in an uncertain economic environment, there is a lack of intellectual capital (e.g., university graduates) in the startup scene by comparison to the U.S., and there are significant difficulties involved in raising financial capital, which are related to the deficit of intellectual capital and the fragmented ecosystem.

There is, moreover. Also, a disparity between the "fail often, fail fast" mantra bandied around in Silicon Valley and the actual reality of many U.S. entrepreneurs, where failure can be difficult to recognize before it's too late, and venture capital and investors can have an attention span of days, if not hours. The idea that everything "takes off" because it's Silicon Valley, and then the puncturing of this illusion and the dawning realization this is only one side of an entrepreneurial life fraught with challenges and failures, can be even more demoralizing for European Founders already wrestling with other mountains of bureaucratic red tape and a seemingly half-empty investment well.

The best lies are usually those containing a component of truth. "Fail often, fail fast" seems an easy way to describe the inevitable success around the corner if only one has failed enough times, with the phrase completely glossing over the suffering such an ideological approach can inflict and it being unclear what, exactly, enough times is. This being said, failure is inevitable, and it is necessary. It's the ineluctable component of any experience and not just entrepreneurship. The benefit of failure should be seen less as a macrocosm of inevitable triumph "in the end" than as an unending series of lessons leading to a collection of smaller triumphs along the way.

Clearly, where entrepreneurship itself can triumph is precisely by incorporating as much experience as possible, which is a universalising prerogative in its right and not copyrighted by Silicon Valley. And here, Europeans may have their own edge:

Considering the vast diversification of nations, cultures, practices, educational backgrounds, and skills across the European continent, the free movement of intellectual capital across borders, and the increasing entrepreneurial mind-set across generations out of economic necessity, European startups are in a unique position to capitalize on this constellation of circumstances by incorporating as many diverse individuals as possible into their enterprise. This enables an aggregation of organic "fail often, fail fast" experiences that have contributed to the tool kits of individuals from all walks of life, considerably broadening the operational horizon of the startup and enriching its ideas. From this perspective, the negativity associated with entrepreneurship in Europe is just a front for the negativity of increasingly remaining outside opportunity and getting left behind.

Lesson

You can't let the world's perception of failure rub off on you. You have to learn to create your luck and opportunities, guarantee your success.

4

What Makes People Quit?

Why do people quit, give up or just throw in the towel? Are there times when it makes sense to quit? Are there advantages to quitting or giving in or up? And what are the benefits of standing firm and drawing a line in the sand? Here's my take on these four questions.

Why do people quit, give up or just throw in the towel? Well, maybe they shouldn't have started in the first place. Maybe quitting was just another way of not really starting. I believe the main reason why people quit anything; a job, career, task, goal or relationship is because they no longer believe that it will never get any better or easier or that they have no longer have control over the outcome(s) Yes, some people lose interest, some people feel they deserve success no matter what they do or don't do. Still, I'm here to tell you that life is a neutral judge. It favors only the brave, humble, courageous, committed and loving. Sure there are examples of people who have succeeded who break all the rules. However, I ask you, do you think their achievements over the long term give them the satisfaction, contentment and peace they desire?

Are there times when it makes sense to quit? Yes. I have abandoned several projects, initiatives or goals over the years that it just didn't make any more sense to pursue due to any number of reasons.

An example of one of such projects was when a group of medical experts joined me and asked if I was interested in partnering with them.

The aim was to establish a pharmaceutical marketing company. They wanted this company to operate on a broader scope,not just advertising but to include creating add ons, finding products, organizing trainings for medical practitioners as well.

The company was successful from day one. We trained a lot of medical practioners, worked with many universities, professors were employed as trainers and consultants. (The Dean of the Munich Marketing University worked with us).

We also managed to win a contract with some of the best Swiss pharmaceutical companies.

Unfortunately, the fairy tale didn't last long. There was a management change in three of our biggest clients. Programs were stopped, and we had to cut costs. They paid penalties, but it was all over. We had to lay a lot of people off.

I invested a lot in the company, and it didn't pay off.

The key is to not quit quickly or easily before you have given your purpose, goal or whatever - adequate opportunities to succeed. No sense in are staying in an abusive relationship or career at the expense of your health or happiness, move on, call it quits and don't beat yourself up about it for years.

Are there advantages to quitting or giving in or up? Yes, but only if you learn from your quitting. Only if you take that learning into your next, goal, mission, purpose or activity.

And what is the benefit of standing firm and drawing a line in the sand? I suggest this action only if whatever it is that you have decided to stick with no matter what, represents your heartfelt dream, passion or purpose in life. I don't care if it takes your entire life to achieve the success you desire and feel you deserve, if you are passionate about it and plan to stick with it no matter what and no matter how long, you will be amazed at the courage, contentment, self-belief, and value you receive from knowing that you stayed the course no matter what the curves, roadblocks or failures along the way.

Motivated by my previous success in the fashion industry, I decided to create my collection. The big idea was to change lingeries into pretty and nice outfits women could wear to clubs and night outs.

I took the step and made drafts and found a lingerie company to design the collection on my behalf. This eventually led to creating a catalog on a boot at the most prominent fashion fair, IGEDO in Europe, located in Düsseldorf.

My boot was a success at the fashion fair, and I had orders from all over Europe; it was more than 5000 pieces.

Here comes the hard part…

I didn't know much about production or the export regulations. I was very intimidated, so I freaked out and sold the business to Triumph international.

This leads me to my next lesson about fear of the unknown.

Fear itself can basically be defined as being The End Result Of A Lack Of Experience. In other words, fear means that we don't trust ourselves to deal with the situation the fear connects to. Take a moment to look at your own life and all the things you're afraid of. How many of them are things you have a lot of experience dealing with? You may have lots of experience being afraid of it, but it's unlikely you have much experience dealing with it.

Fear of the Unknown takes this one giant step further by making us afraid of all the things we don't have experience with. Since, most of us, only have real experience in a limited number of things and situations, it allows the fear to become very, very big. However, as that would be far too much to deal with, our minds transform all of it into one big generalized fear of EVERYTHING. It is this "Generalized Fear" that we have to deal with if we want to become less afraid; or to deal with our fear of the unknown.

Unfortunately, because the fear was transformed into a Generalized Fear it doesn't connect to "things" any more. Typically, to deal with a fear, we would work to gain experience with the thing we're afraid of. A fear of snakes would allow us to start working with a picture of a snake, working our way up to using a rubber snake, and then finally touching a real, non-poisonous snake. However, because the Generalized Fear doesn't connect to any "thing" we can't just work with it to overcome the fear.

While it would be technically possible to work with "unknown things" to deal with the fear since it is a fear of the unknown, any thing we use would have little meaning, this is because we aren't afraid of the "thing" as much as we are so scared of our inability to deal with it. However, this actually tells us what we need to do in order to overcome our "Fear of the Unknown" - Teach ourselves that we are capable of dealing with everything.

In general terms, capability is the ability to deal with anything and everything that comes our way. It doesn't require that we succeed at dealing with them, only that we have the ability to try. It is this that we need to develop in our own lives if we want to be able to overcome our fear. Once we become capable human beings, we no longer need to be afraid that we can't deal with "whatever happens." That means we have no more reason to be afraid of the things we don't have experience with.

This isn't to say that we won't still have fear in our lives. There are many more types of fear than just the generalized fear of the unknown. However, the ability to be Capable in your own life will still lessen all the other fears. So, instead of being afraid any longer, put that effort into becoming more Capable.

How to Get Over Your Fear of the Unknown

Do you constantly fear what is about to come in your future? Do you fear the unknown? Do you procrastinate as a result of that? Fear not – is going to make you overcome your fear of the unknown.

First of all, you don't have to worry as you venture into the unknown. You can take tiny steps every day towards your goals. They don't have to be big ones—start small and slow.

As you leave your comfort zone out into the unknown territory, tell yourself: I can figure it out as I get along. I don't have to know everything. Repeat this statement several times every day until you completely believe it. Life gets easier and you are more aware and alert.

You overcome your fear of the unknown by overcoming the supreme fear of your life, which is fear of death. If you can overcome this fear, you will never be scared of anything.

So how do you overcome your fear of death? By doing bold deeds and confronting upright whatever comes your way without hesitating or procrastinating. Be in Do-Die missions and come out as a winner many times. Of course, you will die some of the times as well. You will know what it is like to die and then bounce back to life.

That brings confidence into the equation. Yes, you need to develop confidence. You need to believe in yourself and experiment by trial and error. When you know how something which you are interested in works, everything falls into place, it is your passion and drive. It can happen at first be a part-time job but eventually you make it full-time.

You need to ask yourself constantly: Does it meet the requirements of today? Is there an easier way to do it? Do I have the right skills? How can I improve my skills? Is it helping me? Is it helping others?

Once you have exercised the questions and found the answers and taken the required actions accordingly, who can stop you? Your fear of the unknown territory vanishes because now you know a lot in your niche.

That is not the end however. Because to keep up with the modern day, you need to be constantly up-to-date, research on the web and ultimately learn, grow and take further actions. That is how you stand out from others and your fears, if any, disappear in a blink.

Before you know it, people are talking about you and your products and purchasing them in bulks and you know then, you have made a name for yourself. How much better could life get?

Lessons

People quit most times out of fear. You have to learn to overcome fear by believing in yourself and achieving sheer determination.

5

What is Failure culture, and why do we avoid it?

There's a trend in the corporate world where it's easier to point others or blame circumstances when it comes to talking about our challenges. Admitting mistakes openly with colleagues or managers is not a common practice, mainly because of the fear of being criticized, blamed or even fired.

This collective behavior, known as Psychological Danger, translates into a lack of failure culture, a culture afraid of trying, where transparent, healthy and efficient communication don't usually succeed. In consequence, the health of the working environment is hugely affected, limiting creativity and innovation.

On the contrary, Psychological safety is a shared belief that the team is safe for interpersonal risk-taking. It can be defined as "being able to show and employ one's self without fear of negative consequences of self-image, status or career."

Teams that work in this circumstances understand the importance of failure culture, sharing it and its positive impact on the operations. Research shows that psychological safety allows high-performance teams to unleash their potential, making companies more agile, strategic and innovative—this leads to fulfilled and productive teams and, as a result, happier individuals.

Everyone you work with is human. Everyone will make a mistake—probably a lot of them. And every company you've heard of and looked up to works with humans and failures. How your company responds to failures is critically important.

First, let's define what is and isn't a reasonable failure. Stealing money, knowingly breaking the law, and conscious dishonesty are not reasonable failures. A reasonable failure is when something doesn't go as expected or hoped, but the company can and will recover, and has maintained its morals. Unreasonable failures are when an employee has acted immorally, against their own better judgment, or purposely done ill to the company or others.

Most failures, then, are actually reasonable. Too often, otherwise reasonable failures are treated like they are not reasonable—and therefore unacceptable.

The Cost of Not Allowing Reasonable Failures

From failure, we learn. Innovation often comes as a result of failure. When is dealing with changing and even complex environments, industries, technology and customer needs, it's rare we "get it right" the first time. Demanding we get it right the first time limits the likelihood we'll learn from the experience—learning which usually results in growth and innovation—resisting reasonable failure will cost you.

Morale

The first casualty of overly punishing reasonable failures is morale. Teams become divided as the safety of the individuals is threatened, and collaboration declines. Studies have found that work pressure can trigger the fight-or-flight response—making us feel that we are in a life or death situation—Coming into work becomes exhausting. Soon, your best employees start leaving.

Retention isn't the only impact of declining morale. The research firm Great Place to Work found that organizations with happy employees have 3x the revenue growth compared to companies that don't. Employee safety is important to your bottom line.

Delivery speed

Delivery speed suffers as employees spend more and more time trying to politically cover themselves or distance themselves from failures than building value for the customer. Employees will be less proactive in addressing problems, since taking any unsanctioned action means that they are absorbing the risk if the action is deemed a failure.

Decision making

Similar to delivery speed, the speed at which decisions are made down. Quite often, bureaucracy is a response to failure. Someone bought something they should have, so now all purchases have to have two signatures—that one failure has now slowed every subsequent purchase. So, next week when buying an external tool will help deliver the product faster, your team is chasing signatures instead of results.

This happens not just with purchases, but all types of decisions. Consider if all architecture questions must go through committee.

Lost innovation

Innovation requires creative thinking, which requires safety. Innovation should sound like "what if we…" or "could we try…." If the effort of asking permission is too great and requires the possibility of backlash for a failure, employees stop asking the questions that lead to new discoveries. If you aren't allowed to fail, you can only ask questions to which you already know the answers. You won't be able to progress beyond what you already know.

Customer experience

Simon Sinek, an author and expert on leadership, tells of an experience boarding a plane where someone was treated horribly by a gate attendant. When he asked why she was treating them like that, she responded, "Sir if I don't follow the rules, I could get in trouble or lose my job."

Simon goes on to say that her mistreatment of customers was because she didn't feel safe and don't trust her leaders. A fear of failure for your employees will translate to an inability to properly serve your customers. A pleasant customer experience often relies on an employee being able to make decisions. Some of those will fails, cost more than expected, or have other repercussions. But most will reward customers and build trust and loyalty.

Two Different Concepts of Failures

It strikes me that we use quite different definitions of failures when we talk about learning from them on the one hand and failure prevention as well as correction on the other—Because on the one hand, failure means deviation from a standard or rule. We have defined, or even negotiated with customers, the requirements that our product or service should meet and specified the relevant features. If we deviate from this or have overlooked functionally relevant requirements, failures would occur. Of course, we can and should draw learning and improvement impulses from this.

On the other hand, we make assumptions and decisions with uncertain outcomes, are subject to errors, conduct experiments, and test hypotheses. In retrospect, some then speak of mistakes, of wrong decisions even. Surgeons gruffly call this "postmortem smart-assing," because afterward, it is easy to have known better beforehand. The English term "failing forward" excellently describes the culture of experimentation, in which one dares to do something that may or may not lead to the goal. We often only know because we dare to make mistakes, to reject hypotheses, to make uncertain decisions or decisions with uncertain outcomes. I would therefore never call these disproved hypotheses and decisions leading to unintended effects failures or wrong choices.

Three Distinct Subcultures

I recognize three significant subcultures. First is the subculture of failure avoidance with an attitude of "Do it right the first time" (Philip Crosby). It is characterized by planning, standardization, discipline in adhering to rules and standards, and forward-looking action, as well as by acting with personal and collective responsibility.

It is the subculture of experimentation with an attitude of "failing forward" (John Maxwell) secondly. It is characterized by the joy of experimentation, the willingness to make and recognize mistakes, to reject theses, to revise one's own decisions and to respect this in others—Such a culture is an important basis for the ability to innovate.

Thirdly, there is the subculture of continuous improvement with an attitude of "higher, faster, further" (Henri Didon). It is characterized by measuring and analyzing, by ambition and the common pursuit of improvement.

The subcultures of failure prevention and continuous improvement are very compatible and can easily coexist. But the subculture of experimentation is mostly not good and not easily compatible with them. I cannot coherently demand "avoid" mistakes and "make mistakes" at the same time. And continuous improvement as well as innovation are also very fundamentally different. What does this mean for companies, which generally want and need to pursue all three thrusts? How do we get a good "as-well-as" of these cultures, rather than an "either-or"? First of all, it is important to distinguish between these subcultures and their underlying misconceptions in the first place, in terms of content and language. Not everyone in the company has to belong to all three subcultures. Accordingly, it is advisable to differentiate according to roles: people in charge of process, improvers, and innovators. Then, it is important to create and promote a high level of mutual appreciation among these role holders. This requires the innovators' appreciation for the process runners' rule discipline and the improvers' small-step approach. And it requires their appreciation for the innovators' disruptive, experimental, revisionary approach. This does not complete the creation of advanced failure cultures, but at least, it creates the necessary prerequisite.

Managing Failure Culture

It's inevitable that people make mistakes. Often, the impact of these mistakes are high — sometimes, it breaks other team's code, introduces regressions which can lurk around for a long time. On large projects, especially where a good chunk of legacy is in play, mistakes happen more often and are way more harder to find.

You can also make a mistake by having the wrong idea; you stick to it, pour more and more of your (and others') energy into it, and it turns out not being a solution to your problem.

At the end of the day, you will fail as everyone else, and you have to be able to make that failure applicable, so it can contribute to your next success.

The Blame Game

Probably you heard these a plenty times:

"I've told this a thousand times but people are still doing it!"

"Great, another three months of work thrown out the window."

and my personal favourite: "Who will take the responsibility for this?"

If the lack of accountability and blame game are recurring themes on your retrospectives, your organisation might have a problem with handling failure. These two issues may seem contradictory but, in fact, they go hand in hand and amplify each other.

Suppose people see that mistakes are left unhandled. In that case, they will call each other out on it — probably not the most polite way, out of frustration, doing a lot of collateral damage in the process. When people expect to be blamed and pilloried for making mistakes, they are more likely to avoid admitting their mistakes and thus learn from them.

The culture won't change by talking about it. What you can do is start acting on it and believe that others will follow.

How Agile Development Helps Dealing with Failure
Agile development methods focus on people, adaptability and of course quality. Learning from failures are not just an option, but a core part of the methodology. Every mistake is an opportunity to adapt, and they have to be taken care of in a way to get the most value out of them. If they are handled properly, failure can be just as valuable as success.

Trust
We trust people to deliver. It doesn't mean we're not prepared for someone failing but if it happens, we trust that we will learn from the failure and adapt.

Transparency

Transparency is a core value of agile development. Responsibilities are clearly defined, progress is clearly communicated and each and every one's work must be visible for team members and external stakeholders. In a genuinely agile workflow, "getting away" with a mistake cannot be possible.

Continuous Feedback

Breaking down the work to bite-size chunks and delivering working software as frequently as possible limits the impact of a failure and allows us to adapt quickly.

Retrospective

Regularly reflecting on how the team operates gives us the opportunity to learn from our mistakes and adjust our processes to make sure that the mistake won't happen again.

Minimum Viable Value

When is trying out new ideas, it's essential that we concentrate on delivering the MVV that's enough to test the validity of the idea. In case of the idea turns out to be invalid or not feasible, we can limit the amount of sunk costs by getting that information as soon as possible.

How to Handle Failure in a Constructive Way

If You are the One to Blame

You made a mistake. It might be a pretty banal one. Somehow, it all the way through, wasting others' time / went to production / disrupted the work of another team. Shit happens.

Whether you discovered your own mistake or someone else did, take ownership. Open, a bug report, talk to your boss, and fix it ASAP. Be honest about how did the mistake happen. Most importantly, identify what can you do different in the future to avoid making the same mistake again. It's not just for you: others can learn from your experience as well.

Be proactive and find ways to catch mistakes like this in the future. Maybe a new tool could help to catch this earlier or the working agreement should be extended. Be sure to bring up the issue on your next retrospective.

What you should not do is to shift blame to others. Yes, you made the mistake, but it passed the review and testing! They also made a mistake! Perhaps they did, but it doesn't make your mistake smaller. Leave the dealing with their part of the responsibility to them, and concentrate on your own.

On the other hand, if you see someone taking responsibility and you also feel responsible, join the discussion and elaborate how you could do your part better.

It's worth it. Admitting your mistakes not just helps you and your organization to learn, but it also helps you to keep your integrity and build your character. No wonder why great people are doing it.

If You are the One Who Blames
You found a nasty bug. Turns out to be a rookie mistake, or even worse, blatant ignorance. You can't imagine making such mistake because you're one of the 90% who's above the

average. Your day is ruined because you spent time cleaning up someone's mess instead of doing something useful.

First of all, give yourself time to calm down. Then, try to reach the person privately: give them a chance to take ownership of their mistake and manage it according to to the previous section. If it doesn't work, talk to their manager or a senior member of their team.

Don't start with gathering evidence and writing an essay about what went wrong, you're not going on a trial. You're not just wasting your own time with it, but creating an atmosphere where the other will feel like they need to defend themselves instead of taking ownership of their mistake.

Of course, if you have some constructive thoughts, it's ok to publish them on a broader forum, but do it with diligence and only after you tried talking to the "offender" privately first. And never do it in a way that the affected person is not involved and cannot participate in the discussion.

While failure in the past was taboo, today it has become really popular. Changes are so sudden and vertiginous, that if a product takes two years to go the market, it is already obsolete. Overcoming the fear of failure is one of the skills that leaders need to develop to facilitate a culture of innovation

Why we avoid failure culture
Each of us responds to stress and fear differently. Some are motivated by fear; others are paralyzed. And our response also varies according to to the context. If we want to maintain the

status quo, we should better not stress out proposing new ideas or uncovering issues.

People tend to avoid doing things that can negatively influence how others perceive their competence. This a form of self-protection, though it can impact negatively how people interact in a team. People who do not feel psychological safe avoid proposing ideas or speaking up if they notice a problem in the process.

We are afraid to fail or be perceived negatively because we do not want to risk what we have. A new idea could be mind-blowing and start a chain reaction. Being the first can be good, but the consequences sometimes can be scary too. It must have been scary to be the Copernicus that placed the Sun rather than the Earth at the center of the universe. Edison failed 999 times until the first light bulb worked at try #1000. In these cases, they were one-person entrepreneurs, but what happens when we are part of a company, or even within a family? We tend to stay quiet and avoid risky proposals to maintain the status quo and reduce the suffering of being rejected or punished.

Failure is the new status quo

Fear of failure causes more pain than failure itself. It affects all other activities that one performs, and can even become a self-fulfilling prophecy. We suffer more because we are not doing what we want, or because we are doing it, but halfway, to avoid more future suffering. While, in reality, much of what we want to avoid is just multiplied x 10 in our minds. We just think about what is the worst that can happen, and we do not see the best that can happen.

Besides, the way in which entrepreneurs react to failure, make our employees react in similar ways, we are role models. Sometimes, we not only avoid proposing ideas, but we discourage others to do it. We are afraid that others will make us look bad, either because their idea doesn't work, or because it is too revolutionary and we didn't think of it before.

As entrepreneurs, we have to demystify the fear of failing to be able to embrace innovation from anybody in the company. Otherwise, we are mining our chances to do something amazing.

In an interview with Harvard professor Stefan Thomke, Booking.com mentioned that they fail nine times out of 10, so their status quo is to fail. If you are trying new features and testing them in front of the customer all the time, it is more common to fail than not to fail. They don't want to fail, of course, but it is the only way to achieve innovations and changes on their website that will attract the customer faster and better than the competition. In order to achieve this, they are looking to promote a context where people are not afraid to fail. All employees are constantly making changes to the online website until the actual customer visits statistics show what works and what does not.

Brave means that, despite the fear, we have the courage to take action, and that is way more powerful and inspiring than being fearless.

Our mind is set to say more NO than yes. What if we spend more time thinking about what is the best that can happen if we take the risk?

If we are going to fail: fail often, fail fast.
Although it seems counterintuitive, in this age of agile failing quickly is more productive in the long term than seeking perfection, or doing nothing at all. Companies prefer to explore and test as much as possible with the real customer until a positive result is achieved. Making mistakes should no longer be something taboo, but simply an important part of the innovation process. The key is not to fall in love with an idea. If it doesn't work out, go ahead with the next one, Fail often, fail fast. Ideo's slogan, for example, is "fail often to succeed sooner."

Google, for example, says that mistakes to be productive have three characteristics: they are detected quickly, they are not too big to impact the name of the company, and they allow us to learn from the error.

Create a learning culture
Do we want a culture of fear or a culture of learning within our team? To create a learning culture, it is important to demonstrate to the team that:

- Errors, delays or even changes are part of the process. They are not punished. We need to accept that they will happen.

- Communicating when something is wrong as soon as possible is more important than not failing at all

- Blaming or judging someone does not improve the probability of success, it only reduces the probability of generating more ideas in the future, people will not feel safe to speak up.

- Testing has a sole objective, and it is to learn and build something better customized to the customer. If it doesn't work out but we learned, it means we have a better chance to be more successful next time.

- Breakthrough innovations require risk-taking to make them happen. Still, risk-taking can be smart if you use data to support your thinking, train people with discovery-driven skills and build a culture where they feel free to innovate.

Lessons

Encouraging creativity, taking risks, trying new things and being open to new ideas are all keys to organizational success.

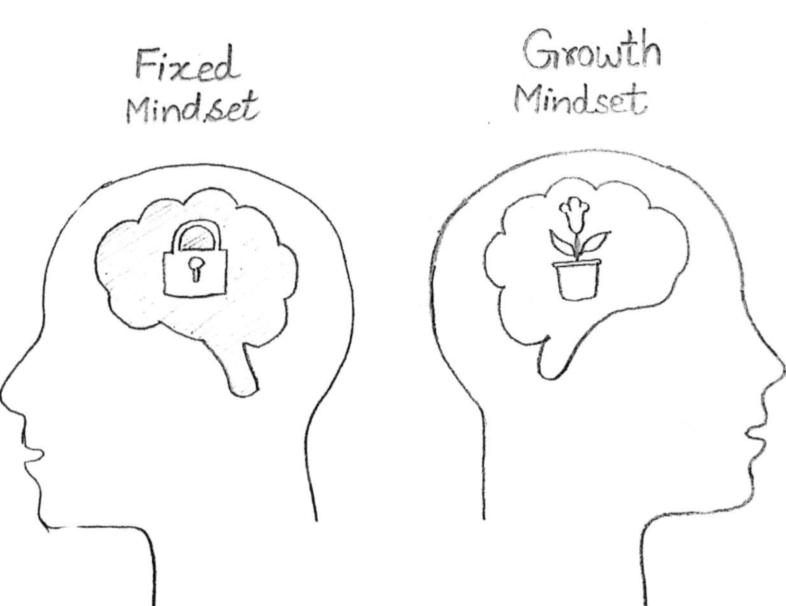

Fixed
Mindset
Growth
Mindset

My-mindguide.com

6

Why We need a Failure Culture

A culture of failure is a set of shared values, goals and practices that encourages learning through experimentation. The goal of building a culture of failure is to create workflows that allow employees to learn from unsuccessful endeavors. Culture of failure has its roots in lean management and is often associated with achieving a culture of innovation.

Instead of fearing or punishing failures, a company that believes in failure-as-an-option (FaaO) recognizes that failure is part of the learning process and that each unsuccessful experiment provides valuable feedback that ultimately can be used to achieve success. By embracing and even seeking out small failures through constant experimentation, each lack of success provides the company with more data to draw upon on when deciding how to move forward.

All successful people have experienced failure. The skill in success is learning from failure and embracing these experiences in a positive way. The Webster dictionary describes persistence as the quality that allows someone to continue doing something or trying to do something even trough it is difficult or opposed by other people.

John C. Maxwell believes that "the difference between ordinary people and achieving people is their perception of and response to failure."

Failure and success is mush like the proverbial rollercoaster of life. To say one has never experienced failure one is not honest with him or her selves. The difference between the average person and a successful person is how he or she managers the failures.

A strategic management philosophy concentrates on long-term goals and if these long-term goals are valid, short-term failure should not affect the desired outcomes. However, if emotion and ones personal self-esteem are effective, one runs the risk of losing sight of the long-term goals.

In today's business world, there are many setbacks and failure whether in one's control or not. Still, the key for personal self-perseverance is the ability to generate personal long-term goals. Understanding Western culture and knowing the high emotional intensity related to both success and failure correlates to many reasons many individuals cannot recuperate from a failure. As with extreme opposite, the ability for an individual to bounce back from a failure is one's personal resiliency to try again. Western culture is extremely difficult to keep emotions focused unless one keeps true to what is important to him or her and realizing if failure is because of a mistake one needs to take this experience, evaluate the reasons for failure, and create a personal case study. The business world spends a large amount of time strategically evaluating their business model and what works best. Individuals also needs to spend enough time evaluating themselves when failure strikes.

Successful people take time in constantly conducting a self-evaluation on their approach and style and understanding their failure and reinventing themselves to achieve success and move beyond failures, catapulting success.

My recommendation is the next time one experiences failure; they need to take the time to celebrate the failure and conduct a review whether individual or with a team, reviewing the failure not as a punitive experience but learning experience. Keep in mind the further one climbs the success ladder the more difficult it becomes to keep from failures.

Some principles to limit failure are prior to taking on a new project. They imply understanding the risks and rewards of the project.

When is evaluating the fundamentals of a project, one must limit the assumptions by using facts and not hearsay information.

Knowing when failure is inevitable is essential to limit loses, and be ready to move ahead with a new project and not second guessing oneself afterwards. This will reduce waste in both human capital and resources.

Prior to any new project, spend the required amount of time in the planning stage. Failure to evaluate and understand the expectations will become counterproductive during the implementation process.

Last and most important, failure, although never the desired outcome, must be celebrated and one must establish the lesson learned from the experience. Individually and socially, loss needs to be understood and an understanding why the project failed.

Leader must take on the responsibility on accepting failure and project a willingness to discuss the failure creating a culture of learning and team.

Lessons

Having a failure culture in organizations and society increases innovation and creativity.
You can't teach people how to succeed without first preparing them how to fail.

SUCCESS
SUCCESS
FAILED
FAILED

My-mindguide.com

7

How to Overcome Failure

Every since the dawn of human history, men have constantly pondered over the many facets of life that surrounded him. The quest for knowledge and ideals of life, though besieged with failures at times, has evolved men into a perfect thinking machine that made his life easier. It presented men with all the comforts of life at his disposal. Though men have reached the ebb of Time -Space quantum with all his knowledge and technology, yet still fails to answer the very fundamental question of human life existence and it's relation to our daily life. Are men really free? Are we free of failure?

You have to understand that life always comes with challenges, and you must be ready to face them. I did, too…

Many of us, myself included, struggle at times with learning from our failures. We sometimes give up as soon as we fail, not realizing that what is necessary is to push a bit harder until we reach a breakthrough.

When I was at Gassner Beckmann(An advertising Agency) as a partner, This is one of the top agencies in Munich and has a lot of big clients. 4 years went by peacefully until my partner, who owned 50% of the agency and handled the business end, wanted to get rid of me.

He thought that I was too expensive and was not pulling my weight. This led to many legal battles between us, after which he agreed to a settlement to leave the agency. The settlement included a large sum and monthly remunerations. I'm sure he believed that since I had not demonstrated any form of business skills, I was the creative director—the business would inevitably fail, and I would go bankrupt.

Issues Today

Beneath the vast potentialities and abundance, today, man is faced with a vast array of dilemma's; Failure in relationship, failure in career, Financial crises, stress, uncertainty in leading ones life are some core issues which has beset him with the burden of problem-solving complexities towards life.

Today most people don't live their life, rather have lived to the expectation of society, peer groups around them. Although conformity to our surroundings is essential, yet it is not the ultimate. This denies men of free rational thinking and his true freedom. The problem is, we fail to draw a battle line between the expected and what we ought to. Ethics of Life, Morality, and social standard all form a series of unbreakable chain around us, reducing men into a complex dumb machine. The aptitude towards freethinking and unrestrained dynamism is lost within his conditioned perplexities of life. Hence, uneven conformity in the ordeals of life has led to loss of dynamism within men.

Why We Fail And How To Overcome

We fail to perceive why we failed to do. The power of creativity, dynamism, passion, will power is a prerequisite for a complete successful living. Ideas and enthusiasm help a person into doing something creative and innovative things. Difficulties and problems enable us to learn the meaning of life. By overcoming it, we discover our inner strength—we need to be an active window that brings in sunlight instead of a reflecting mirror. Learn to bud discontent at its nib which leads to dissatisfaction, weak will, lost of initiate and dynamism—change things by perceiving things in a different manner. Be positive and face defeat in its eye until it cease to burden you any longer. "Life can only be understood backward, but must be lived forward"-Soren Kierkegaard. Visualize and set priority to one's activities. Cultivate an element of hope instead of fear.

Learn how to live for in learning there is progress. Winners don't do different things but do things differently.

How can you overcome failure? This is a question every student will love to find an answer to. However, when we are talking about failure, it goes beyond just sitting for an examination and failing to meet the requirement. Failure cuts across all spheres of life. It has to do with your career, your business, your marriage and even your friendship.

Failure can be described as lack of success. When there is absence of success in your business or in your career or in the examination you sat for or in your endeavors or in your pursuits or in anything that you do, you have failed. Failure is not a good thing. Therefore, we must find a solid answer to this curious and serious question," how can you overcome failure?" There is a surprising answer embedded in our description of failure. If we described failure as lack of success, what it means in other words is that when you have success you have overcome failure. This shifts our attention to how we can obtain success in whatever we do.

We all know how to do this – fall and get back up. Assuming we know how to walk, which most of us are fortunate enough to do, we went through this specific and miraculous experience ourselves when we were very small.

We've also gone through it in a figurative sense many other times as we move through the ups and downs of life, especially recently. The question isn't whether or not we'll fall; the question is will we be bold enough to get back up again?

A simple principle to attain success is what I described as the 3DA. The three Ds stand for Dedication, Determination and Discipline while the A stands for Attitude. This was the principle Jesse Owens adopted at the 1936 Olympics Games in Berlin, where he won four gold medals. He broke nine Olympic records and tied two. You can also cling to this principle and earn for yourself victory over failure; you can also hold on to this nugget and obtain for yourself enviable success.

Let's look closely at this principle, describing its components one after the other. The first one I am going to discuss is dedication.

Dedication is such a vital tool we need for climbing the ladder of success that it speaks more volumes than what we thought it is all about. The first thing that should come to your mind when you are about to commence whatsoever in this life is your readiness to devote your time and resources to achieve the goal of the task and that is exactly what dedication is all about. Dedication is closely followed by hard work. You literally tell yourself, "If truly I am dedicated to this course I am ready to give it all it takes." What does that mean? It means hard work is swing to action.

The second tool I will be discussing is determination. Sometimes, I find it difficult to differentiate determination from dedication. But I will use this simple illustration to describe the relationship and difference between faith and determination. When a student is through with college education or secondary school, what's next? He starts thinking of how to get into the tertiary institution in order to build on his educational career. Let's look at success as an educational career, therefore just like tertiary education is sequel to college education or secondary school, so determination is sequel to dedication. I will love to say that determination is persistent dedication. Just like this proverb tells us, "everyone is eager to play the piano but few are willing to carry it on." These few people are the dedicated and determined individuals. Have you ever heard the quotation of Michael Smurfit that says, "Never accept failure, no matter how often it visits you. Keep on going. Never give up". That is determination!

The next tool for success I will be talking about is discipline. Congratulations, you are now dedicated and determined.

Please, don't get too excited. Success wants you to have control over yourself, feelings and your dealings. I mean you! There are times you are hungry and you need something to eat but you know eating is not the best thing to do at the moment. You need to control yourself—that's discipline. Discipline will hold you and make you be in charge when you are on your journey for the pursuit of success.

I want to note at this point that I was happy in my role as a creative director; I needed neither a suit nor tie, and I was enjoying the casual dressing but, at that point, I had to be determined and take the bull by its horns by playing the part of a business owner and looking the part. I got some blazers, and ties took on both the creative and business roles. Contrary to what my ex-partner thought, the agency grew, and my ex-partner went broke after a couple of months.

Last but not the least, let's look at this important component needed for success, it is called attitude. Someone has said," your attitude determines your altitude in life." I think I so much agree with the person. The interesting thing about attitude is that it is a two sided thing; it can be positive or negative. The positive will take you up while the negative will bring down. The positive will bring you success, joy and fulfillment while the negative will hand you failure, sorrow and shame. The people who are ready for success are those who have the right attitude. They are people with the right opinion towards success. So, like Jesse Jackson, I will say, "If I can conceive it and believe it, I can achieve it. It's not my aptitude but my attitude that will determine my altitude with a little intestinal fortitude." This same attitude is what handed Jesse Owens four gold medals in a record breaking Olympic game that gave him a place in the book of history.

Lessons

It would help if you had determination, dedication, discipline, and attitude to overcome failure. They are the building blocks of a successful life.

8

How to Turn Your Failures into Massive Success

If you have failed at anything in life you are able to achieve massive success. This may sound like a strange statement but it is very true.

As I have mentioned before,

I've had my share of massive failures; I remember one of them to be when I was one of the first in Germany who started with Product Placement in Movies and TV.

So I worked with big movie-companies – I hired also an Expert who was in the Movie/Film scene. The business startet great. We had contracts –

With Coca Cola, Burger King, Ice. And so on.

The movie companies wanted the money – but weren't reliable to fulfill the contracts. They cut the product shots out after the Presentation also.

Bad reputation for me – I closed the company after 18 months of operation.

Some of the most significant success stories you will ever hear come from failures. After all, a failure is only what you perceive it to be. If you think it is the end of the world, then it is, but if you think it's an opportunity, then it will be. Here are a few ways to turn your failures into massive successes.

1. **Focus on the solution.**

It's so easy so focus on what when wrong but success can often be found in finding the solution to your failure. By focusing on the solution, you are keeping a success mentality and will be better prepared to recognize success when it presents itself.

I don't know about you, but sometimes, when I'm faced with a problem, especially one that I don't think belongs to me, but is suddenly mine to resolve, my inner two year old has a tantrum.

Successful people know that, when faced with a problem, they should spend 80% of their time on finding the solution and 20% on the problem. The rest of the population reverses the percentages and spends most of their time being irritated at the problem they face.

What if you could spend the majority of your time focusing on the solution instead of the problem, how would your life be different, what would it look like?

In addition to focusing on the solution rather than the problem, another way to increase your chances of success and increase your confidence when you find yourself in a similar situation is to change your mental focus. The fastest way to do this is to change the questions you're asking yourself. Instead of asking yourself, "what happens if I fail at this, what if I can't come up with a solution?" ask yourself, "What's the best way to get this done and enjoy the process?"

What if you could do both these things when faced with a problem, how would your life be different, what it look like?

2. **Learn, learn, learn.**

Failure is only failure when you don't learn from it and apply what you have learned. You are doomed to repeat your failures if you never learn from them. You never know what one learning experience from a failure can do to help you succeed beyond your wildest dreams.

- **Learn From Failure**

Since you're trapped, for the time being, on a planet full of gravity and other irresistible forces, you're going to fail at one time or another. Whether or not you fail is simply a matter of time, not "if." How you harness your failure is a better question. When others fail around you - to meet expectations or other standards - the question remains: what do you do with their failure? Do you recover from failure? What can you learn from failure?

I once met a guy who was the sales manager of Nintendo and had very good connections to leading drugstore companies in

Germany. I came up with the idea that we could create "Traffic-generators" for the drugstore shops. We would place displays with creative merchandise in the stores and advertise them for a good price. The concept was designed in a way that shoppers would come into the store looking for the merchandise and on their way out would take some random drugstore products. So – generating more traffic and increasing sales.

We tested the idea extensively and it worked out. We got a big contract and pushed ourselves to place 20.000 displays each month. We were making much money. We felt like kings of merchandise. Then, out of the blue, the phones started ringing, and the shops wanted to send their unsold merchandise back to us. What? I learned later that my partner signed a secret deal that guaranteed a buy back.

Many bike helmets were flocking in, I mean truckloads full of merchandise, we had to rent space. Eventually, we made a deal and stopped everything all together. We managed to keep some money and closed the company without going bankrupt.

Did I learn from my mistakes? Absolutely. Failure is an opportunity to gain greater skill and mastery. In all areas of life.

Want to know how to learn from failures? Your journey starts this second. The fact that you're reading this article is proof that you're prepared to take on the challenges that you might not want to face. It takes courage for people to realize that they need help on how to learn from failures. And you, my dear friend, have that. Learn from your mistakes and move on with your life starting with these steps.

Humility Helps.
A little bit of humility goes a long way. You know you did something wrong; and while you might be feeling a bit defensive, you had best keep your emotions in check. Accept that your plans don't go as well as you would have wanted and apologize to those who warrant your apology.

Humility is the first step to mending broken ties and relationships. Ignore other people who are talking about you behind your back—whom you were before, or whatever your status might have been—those are no longer significant. This is not the time for you to start another war, but the time for you to reflect on what you have done.

Observe And Report.
By now, the ruckus should have died down a little. If you want to learn from failures, then you need to stay quiet and start listening to other people for once. Watch how your peers and colleagues are handling matters. You might not have noticed these things before; but now that you're gave the chance to observe them, you might be able to pick up a thing or two. This is your chance to learn how you can help straighten things out.

Make Things Right.
If you want to know how to learn from failures, then you'll have to do a bit of dirty work. It's not the most pleasant task to do, especially if it's your mess you're cleaning up; but making things right is extremely crucial to your redemption. If you're

not yet certain of what you can do, ask. You don't have to come up with the one solution that will take care of everything, but you can start by helping out in little ways.

Getting coffee for those who are doing the brunt of the work, for example, is one way you can make amends. Knowing how to learn from your failures is very important. This is the only way you can grow as a person. Whether it's your career or your personal relationship on the line, you must still learn from your experiences.

As much as we would all love to live an easy life with endless resources and finances, most people might admit that life would be pretty monotonous if there were no obstacles or failures. Evidence of this might be seen by watching the celebrity gossip television programs, where the rich and famous of Hollywood seem to bounce from one crisis to another, seemingly bored of living the good life. How many times have you watched such stories in the news, and thought what you would do to benefit humanity if you could have their vast resources of wealth, power and influence? How many times have you been puzzled when trying to understand their mindset?

Success caused without any hard labor or without crossing any insurmountable barrier is hardly remembered even by the most successful people. To compare it with something which we experience every day, we would not value sunlight if it was not snatched by darkness of the night. At the same time, no one in this world is spared from ill fortunes and his share of bad luck, disappointments and failures, what separates men from mouse is the individual ability to deal with failures. While some succumb to their past rejections and present failures, some rise above it and strive harder to perfect their processes to achieve success. The second group always visualizes the entire spectrum of life—with its due quota of ups and downs—and sees every failure as another opportunity thrown at them which has the potential of future success. This relentless pursuit of happiness and success despite all the hurdles which might come in the way, eventually take these people high on the ladder of accomplishment. The people who are tormented at the sheer thought of failure, past or present, are usually left behind.

What is it that makes successful people look beyond their set backs and re-set their goals with renewed enthusiasm and vigor? Here are some of the ways by which people can achieve this skill:

- Treat the past as over and future as illusive. This means you have to act for the present moment, which is all that you have in front of you. If you let your past failures come in your way of thinking positively for the future, you would be perennially haunted by what obstacles may occur in future. The key is to treat any set-back as an opportunity to improve the way you do things. Once you start believing in what the present is offering you, you tend to be more focused on making the most of your opportunities.

- Believe in yourself. We all know about the rejection which Graham Bell faced from the scientific community when he invented a new way in which we could communicate. If Bell had given up on his belief and resigned to his failures, we would have perhaps never reached this far as we have today in the field of communication. Failures, negative criticism, set backs are all intrinsic part of success. If you believe in your ideas and can firmly stand by it, you can look at every failure on its face and see the sun that shines behind the barrier.

The talent or ability to take every failure in the stride is an important asset in any organization. It is the leader's responsibility to coach his employees and team members of the importance of remaining steadfast in their approach to achieve respective career and personal goals. Set backs would come and go and would continue to do so, so long as you are involved in some kind of activity in life. There is a saying that, when it rains, it pours. Nothing can be truer than this saying when it comes to being flooded with set backs, where we go wrong is that we fail to notice the silver lining around the cloud.

- **Re-Define Failure**

Too often, it seems people allow failures to define them. They are identified with their failure: as lazy, drunk, liar, cheat, bully...whatever the adjective, it's tied to their failure. Instead, take control and re-define the failure. People are people, after all. Failure is something that's going to happen to the best of people from time to time.

Through my agency, I had contacts in the first commercial TV stations in Germany. They needed business and content so I offered them a deal: Pay Per Order. So I didn't need to invest money in advertising. Also, I managed to find hotels in Europe who wanted to sell their cold beds in the low season.

I created a lot of promotional material, we shot commercials with my wife as the presenter. The commercials were aired day and night. We set up a call center and my staff answered the phones: direct booking.

We sold a lot of tickets for 99 Deutsche Mark each, this was the nice part. Now, we had to learn the travel business. Hotels weren't honoring the vouchers; they didn't stick to the terms of the contracts. Eventually, stranded travelers camped out in front of our office. It was a nightmare, My organizational skills weren't that great, so I ordered software, hired new people, dealt with the hotels, and saved the business, but issues kept springing up. After 3 years of struggling with this, I closed the business—paid back a lot of vouchers and nobody was left behind.

There was a silver lining though, I was now an expert in Travel direct marketing and big travel companies invited me to share my experience. 2 years later the first last minute was born – copying my concept.

Re-define failure as an opportunity to learn from a mistake or poor choices that you or another make. It's a free education, and it costs nothing to witness mistakes and learn from them. Re-defined this way, failure becomes a learning experience and genuine growth opportunity every time.

- **Put Failure to Work For You**

It's sort of like being the new kid in school, and the bully upper-level students want to get your goat. They cajole, bully and mock away...but if it doesn't matter to you much, then you've stolen their thunder. When, a bully, has the upper hand and knows he's got it, then he has control over you. If he can't have that control, then he's nothing but a nuisance.

This same holds true for the power of failure - except you can actually harness the negative "vibe" and put it to work for you. Learn how to make your failure, or that of another, work for you. Don't get mad at the fact that you've loused up - take notes.

What caused it? Is it a pattern? How can I prevent this? What have I learned?

When others assume this failure defines you, seize the moment and make that day the re-defining moment you decide you're not doing this again. Decide you aren't going to fail like others have, and be re-defined. Strengthen yourself and adapt: Recover from failure when you learn from failure.

Put failure to work for you to be propelled to become a greater person.

I was propelled to make better decisions with all I learned from my failures.

I was asked to teach visual branding on the Advertising academy in Munich and also on the University Munich. It was really a pleasure to teach ambitious students how to create visual brand value.

The work was fun – but also very time consuming, because I took it serious. I had to prepare my lectures, correct the exams and sit on the final exams. The payout was little, but I got the chance to empower the incoming generation.

- **Fail Fast and Get Back On the Horse!**

You can learn a lot in a rodeo. One of the better examples of failing properly is when a cowboy or cowgirl gets bucked off a bronco, and gets right back in the saddle. This idea holds water for any situation, including failure.

History is replete with figures who've tried and failed, but then tried again after learning the tough lessons. Every great invention, company, government or historical figure is fraught with either genuine or apparent failure - and these folks have learned to get right back in the saddle. Great people have this in common - they learn from failure. They get the hard knocks and recover from failure, fast.

It's not about how hard you've fallen, nor about who you let down, or about who let you down when they've failed - it's about what you've learned from it and how quickly you get back on the horse that really define you.

If you fail properly, you won't fail again. You'll just be upgrading

3. **Focus on the future.**

Failure has an amazing way of making you focus on the past and have regret in life. If you live in shame and the past, you will never be able to seize all the opportunities that lay ahead of you. The greatest thing for you to do is start to look to the future and how you can use those failures to help you succeed. If you focus on the future, you can't be stuck in the past.

In truth, it's quite compelling to focus on the past. Whether we're resting on our laurels for prior accomplishments or berating ourselves for past mistakes, there is a certain ease of familiarity about days gone by. Been there, done that. It may not be exciting anymore but, hey, it's what we know.

The problem is that staying rooted in the past makes it awfully difficult to forge ahead. You simply can't look backward and forward at the same time. While it's perfectly okay and even advisable to reflect on past achievements and errors, you just cannot allow yourself to remain mired in your own history. The way to move forward is, well, to move forward. Chart a course and start sail. Take in all the wonders that lie ahead. Steer clear of the hazards. With both eyes focused on what's before you, you can make sound decisions and take meaningful steps toward achieving your goals.

Lessons

To turn your failures into success, you have to be focused and ready to learn from your mistakes. Observe what works and doesn't; don't give up trying new things.

9

Consistency: A key to success

How many of you can claim with absolute certainty that you have applied consistency and persistence in your daily life with some measure of success?

Consistency and persistence are two elusive virtues difficult to sustain if not regularly engaged. Let's take a moment to peer through the lens of what consistency and persistence have to offer.

You've no doubt been well informed of the merits of consistency within a practical approach. Attend any weekend course and I can assure you the instructor will endorse the power of consistency as a key attribute toward accomplishment.

Consistency may be defined as developing discipline in a chosen field, in favour of a favourable outcome. Those who uphold discipline are rewarded with success since they have harnessed enduring focus through concerted effort.

Let's be clear while on the subject. Success in this context is not limited to certain areas of life. If losing weight and eating healthy is your primary goal, taking appropriate action steps on a frequent and consistent basis may be considered a success.

Far too many people discount the power of consistent effort towards their goals. Consistency creates powerful neural networks in the brain known as grooving. These grooved neural networks help form strong connections within the brain's synaptic connections, thus enhancing your concentration on a task or goal.

When one applies intermittent effort to a goal, the brain does not receive sufficient stimuli to form powerful habits. It is the Hebbian theory, introduced by the Canadian psychologist Donald O. Hebb who states that "nerves that fire together, wire together." With consistent effort, your brain acquires permanent neural connections as a result of prolonged application.

Consistently focussing attention towards your goals allows the brain to lock on to the target. Consistency may be perceived as the ability to sustain continuous effort despite external forces. Ceaseless determination is paramount in order to draw a favourable outcome.

Consistency builds character and sharpens the mind. Consistent people are triumphant. They possess an inner drive which is unyielding. They are firm in their resolve to bring about positive results. They do not compromise by cutting corners or taking the road less travelled—ultimately, this dedication pays off with the rewards that await.

One final thought on consistency worth mentioning. Consistency is essential in a task-orientated goal since it allows you to trace your results through to completion. For example, many people give up on improving their nutritional and exercise goals as challenges arise.

Following success without, a measure of sustained performance is likely to produce ineffectual outcomes. In a number of instances, one's desired results may not be visible for some time, particularly when modifying nutritional and exercise goals. Oftentimes, events are working in your favour albeit behind the scenes, while laying the foundations for future progress.

When it comes to business, consistency is absolutely a key to success. Becoming and staying as consistent as you need to be to achieve your goals is not always easy but it is a behavior that anyone involved in business would do well to learn and apply.

The truth is that more businesses fail than succeed. Statistically, the odds of any new business actually 'making it' and becoming profitable enough to sustain itself are slim. But how can you overcome the odds? What can you do to propel your business to a place where it can not only be successful, but also grow and prosper? To accomplish success on this level, you need to embody several behaviors and habits, but one of the most crucial of these is consistency.

If you can learn to be consistent, then your talent can be fully realized and your ideas can be given a fair chance of working. You would be amazed at how many businesses, started by talented and intelligent people, fail because they neglect to continue in their good habits, day in and day out. A lot of factors come into play, but there is no substitute for being determined, reliable, and consistent.

Becoming the 'Model Of Success'
One of the key concepts to understand as it relates to consistency, lies in the idea that you need to 'become what you desire to become.' In other words, don't just hope that your business will succeed. Instead, start living it on a day to day basis. Embody your ideas to the point where you make them real. When you believe in you and in your business enough, you can only succeed!

Suppose your company was really busy and successful, then you would most likely need to do things a certain way to generate that result and outcome. But for a new startup, for a business that has not grown to that point yet, or even for a company that is older but hasn't grown a whole lot in past years... a lot can be accomplished by, for example, showing up to work and putting in the hours that you would be required to put in if your business were incredibly busy and successful.

Being consistent in a way as simple as showing up to work, day in and day out, is often overlooked. Many people do not realize how much good a consistent presence on their part can do for their business, even if they have employees who can manage things while they are not there. For example, showing up to work and having little in the way of business actually going on might seem like a waste of time. Still, you can utilize down time to further your ideas in other ways, which in turn can help to expand and increase your success to the next level - and we all have a next level. For example, you could work on networking or marketing to grow your client base. You could also get into social media marketing or do more in this area, and utilize that to reach out to possible new clients who can use your products or services.

There is also a need to be consistent in the areas of marketing and advertising, especially as they relate to any online ventures. Consistency in this areas has, time and time again, tied itself to successful businesses. In fact, a lot of successful people have said that it is not actually talent or a natural affinity for leadership that sets a profitable businessman apart from one that is not. The only real common denominator among those on incredibly successful levels is the fact that those who remained consistent in their endeavors, and stuck it out when things got tough, often ended up creating a more profitable business. Overnight success stories might sound fun, but you would be AMAZED at how much went on behind the scenes that the public will never know about. A lot of 'overnight success stories' were only made possible because the businesses involved remained consistent in their day-to-day activities, even when things were not going so well.

The Benefits of Consistency

By remaining consistent, you will be ready to jump at any opportunity that might come along. The restaurant owner, for example, who consistently stays open on Mondays when he is never very busy, could very well find his restaurant the most popular place to eat on Mondays, if he is the only one who, ill commit to staying consistent by staying open on such a slow day. The entrepreneur, who is attempting to market his business online, might be tempted to miss a few blog posts here and there... but if he does, he will cause readers to notice that content is not as 'regular' as it used to be, and this will result in a loss of interest on their part.

Think about the types of businesses that you utilize every day. Where do you buy your groceries? Where do you go out to eat? Where do you buy clothes? Who is your dry cleaner? Have you ever tried to do business with a company that never managed to be reliable? There is nothing more frustrating than needing something, only to realize that the business you planned on using is 'closed' for the day due to 'personal reasons.' This is the kind of inconsistency that will really drag a business down.

In the end, consistency is all about keeping things steady, regular, and reliable. Consistency is going to be one of the most important assets that your business will ever build for itself, and building it will result in increased sales, clients, and success!

If you have been struggling a little bit in the consistency department (as most people do), then I challenge you to put new energy into making your part in your business as reliable and as consistent as you can. Don't misunderstand that consistency means that you are set in your ways and that you never look outside the box to try new things that can help your business grow even more. You will no doubt soon realize how many opportunities such an attitude will open up for you!

Harnessing Persistence

Persistence is defined as the "the act of persisting or persevering..." also "continuing or repeating behavior." It is closely related to words like commitment as well as perseverance. The most successful people in life are always persistent. This is why it is important to cultivate the quality of persistence, no matter what you are aiming for. Of course, there is a clear distinction between the quality of persistence and the term "pesky," which is alternatively defined as annoying. Persistence must always have a purpose or else it will become grating to those practicing and to those listening to the message.

What really is the difference between being persistent and being a royal pain in the butt? Persistence requires a great degree of premeditated thought and advance planning. When someone is persistent, they are fully committed—not to an action, as if repeating multiple incidents with no particular purpose, but to a plan. They believe in a principle and realize that, to achieve their goals, persistence will be required. Someone who is merely repetitive uses this technique as an offensive attack and does so until someone else has the courage to shut them up. Persistence is a far more crafty approach. A persistent person realizes the importance of repetition but is careful about proper timing and using appropriate language. You could say that a persistent person is careful to learn the problem first, creating a plan of action and then sticking to that plan. When problems are discovered, the persistent mind creates alternative routes and adaptable strategies.

Persistence will be required in numerous personal and professional endeavors. Personally speaking, a thinking person realizes that it takes persistence to improve human relationships, whether in the context of friendship, courtship or business. It may not be enough to formulate a good plan if the initial program of action doesn't work, then a persistent thinker will have to come up with another angle. For example, let's say that a relationship is suffering between two people. One person thinks is ill of the other and is unwilling to listen to an apology. If that relationship is worth keeping, then a persistent person will approach the other person with a different strategy. The strategy employed will depend on the other person's personality. Is the other person a co-worker that has a business-oriented mind? Is it romantic partner that appreciates a good sense of humor? If it is a business relationship that you want to form, you may send them an attractive high-heeled shoe with a note about, now that I have a shoe in the door... Knowing personal information or trying humor, the persistent thinker is already at an advantage and well on his or her way to improving those relationships.

Persistence is also important for building faith or adding value to a chosen belief system. It's safe to assume that every belief system is based on a persistent and deliberate influx of knowledge and experience. Professionally speaking, persistence is equally important. New business owners are often times singular proponents of their company and must work twice as hard to establish market and brand name. This requires persistence as there could be many slow months to start with, and plenty of dissatisfied or uninterested customers. New business owners also have to contend with bad news from banking institutions, advertisers and government entities— persistence is vital if you ever hope to succeed in a business.

Persistence is also an important quality for entertainers to learn since rejection and criticism are prevalent in creative fields. Writers and artists must-read rejection slips while actors and singers could be turned away immediately after an audition. Of course, all of this formal rejection is relative to a group of people actually booing you off a performing stage. This is just part of the business and entertainers must learn to be thick-skinned in order to survive in their chosen industry. Other industries are just as competitive and require persistence to stay office politics, job promotions, business development, managerial responsibilities, and corporate takeovers.

I moved to Austria/Kirchberg and founded an agency in my basement. We managed to attract major Austrian companies from Swarovski, Tyrolit to international multi-billion US businesses in the lighting sector, technical fabric, and wood.

These were some of my best and most profitable years. I worked out of the basement with only four employees, and we all performed fantastically. I had my agency in Munich and so I ran back and forth.

Through the power of consistency and persistence, after a year, we rented bigger space and moved the office. It was not the pretty same. There was more space, more people – but not the same intense spirit.

After a couple of years, we moved even in a bigger – very stylish – but again, the spirit never came back. We also did much touristic brands. I hired people like crazy.

In my early 60s, I sold the business and turned a new page in my life book.

In fact, without cultivating the quality of persistence, there is not much for a person to do in the world besides become a follower and allow him or herself to be controlled by the wisdom (and or stupidity) of others. Persistent people make the world turn—they make business grow; they improve worldwide communication and they help to shape this generation's zeitgeist. Why not become a part of this movement? Plan out your future and allow yourself the chance to become everything you aspire to be. Commit to your vision of success and help make the world a better place in your own unique way.

Let us turn our attention now to the power of persistent effort. It should be stated that persistence is a state of mind. It is the hallmark of accomplishment given that persistent people push through pain. Pain refers to the setbacks and roadblocks that are apparent when ploughing ahead. One's ability to recover from failure and setbacks forms the basis for future success.

Persistence acknowledges the existence of external forces continually acting on us. Such forces have the potential to derail or even hinder one's progress. The persistent person acknowledges this forces are working against them, yet lingers ahead.

Behavioral psychologists have long believed that is simply showing up is a sufficient measure towards future success. I hold firm to the belief that showing up is inadequate since people show up every day to dreary and mundane jobs which they loathe. Whilst the body is present, their minds are on vacation somewhere on a tropical island. Showing up means being present and engaged with absolute intention and purpose.

Another key influence is the power of momentum, which is a formidable ally toward goal attainment. Without momentum, one applies partial effort while anticipating victory. Think back to your last project in which you applied persistence and momentum. I daresay that your efforts were met with ease and perfection, as though you were in Flow.

Momentum is the accelerator driving persistence. As you maintain persistence, momentum takes the wheel to hasten progress. Artists will advise you that every creative pursuit takes a life of its own once commitment has been made, compelling it forward.

Persistence is powerful

Persistence means to persist, to keep going despite obstacles or setbacks, to continue moving forward no matter what. Persistence is a powerful force that can be harnessed toward your success. As you probably know, success just doesn't fall into your lap; you have to take action toward success and like climbing a ladder, it takes forward action one step at a time.

Abraham Lincoln is a prime example of persistence in action. Known as one of the greatest presidents in history, Abraham lost eight elections before he finally became president. He also lost his business twice and could have chalked himself up to being a loser, but he didn't. He was persistent and believed he could achieve his dreams.

Another great example is the wonderful children's writer, Dr. Seuss. His book, "And to Think I Saw It on Mulberry Street" was rejected by 27 publishers before finally getting a yes. Many people would have given up after a handful of rejections, but he persisted. Dr. Seuss went on to become one of the greatest children's book writers around, selling more than 200 million copies of his books.

Persistence and passion

If you're passionate about something, chances are you're persistent in moving toward it. Do you have a goal of becoming a published author? Then you'll have to be persistent in your writing and be able to persist even after you get ten or 100 rejection letters for your article or book proposal. I've read about plenty of professional athletes, artists, business owners, etc. that were faced with plenty of setbacks but were determined to be persistence and little by little they edged their way to success.

What is your passion?

Do you have a passion? Were you once passionate about something but have put it on the back burner because things weren't going as fast as you'd like? I admonish you to dig deep and rediscover the passions inside you and make a plan to go forward with persistence toward fulfilling them. It's easier to give up on your dreams than to persist through disappointments and setbacks, but easy won't fulfil you. A sense of ploughing through obstacles, fears and setbacks will fulfill your day in and day out. Knowing that you're set on persisting through ANYTHING to get what you want is a very liberating feeling.

How I developed a passion for brand consulting

The advertising business started to be boring after all those years and times were changing as clients started asking for pitches even for small projects. I was not used to working that way; I was used to working with three year contracts and a monthly remuneration. So I decided that I had to go in another direction. I saw that McKinsey worked for a lot of our clients and how they were treated with much respect as well as their hefty price tickets.

So, I studied Harvard business review and read an article about brand consulting.

I believed in myself that my combination of practical knowledge, creative work, and theoretical background could attract big companies. I worked on a method called brand auditing and pitched my program to old and new clients.

The best years of my career started. Great work, great reputation, impact on companies and people and last but not least travelling around the world and great pay.

The dark side was: personal involvement. I worked like hell. And, of course, I had stuff and assistants but the direct, delicate work, I couldn't delegate. It was fantastic but also very stressful because I always tried to exceed the expectations of my clients.

How to be persistent

Now that you understand that persistence is powerful and necessary, you might be wondering how you can incorporate it into your life. It's not as difficult as you might think. Being persistent is basically committing to not giving up on your goals no matter what happens. It's looking at whatever comes along your path and being determined to deal with it as best as you can so you can continue on your journey toward success.

Sometimes, hurdles come and you're not sure what to do. Know that it's alright. When you don't know what to do, simply do some research to learn how you can handle the situation. There are tools and resources that you can use to learn how to handle different things in life, as well as people who have already faced whatever it is you're dealing with.

Have you come to a halt in your forward progress? Talk to someone else who has been there and get some advice. Are you extremely frustrated or have you given up? Look at your problems in a different perspective, go to a seminar or hire a Life Coach to breathe some new life and dreams into you. Sometimes all it takes is sharing your frustration with someone else to gain fresh insights and revelations.

You can learn to harness the power of persistence to achieve your goals and dreams. Adopt an "I can do it no matter what!" attitude and see how your forward motion picks up speed. It might not always go as planned, but you will move forward. Go ahead and give yourself permission to move forward, soaring on the power of persistence toward fulfilling your passions!

Thus, the power of consistency and persistence are two fundamental forces that have the potential to generate powerful and lasting success in all areas of your life.

Use them wisely.

Lessons

Consistency and persistence are two elusive virtues difficult to sustain if not regularly engaged.
The key to success in life is sustained consistency and persistence.

10

Why is Determination Important For Success?

Determination, one big word that says a lot and is rarely something that happens during the course of business or life in general. Why is this? What stops the average person from getting the important things in their business done? One word—determination. Sometimes, it is easier to pick the low hanging fruit than working on the items that will move you ahead in life.

Determination is a topic that is very near and dear to me. This is the core ingredient to any businesses secret recipe to success or the lack of determination is in the recipe for business struggles. Either recipe, it is there! Determination is all about finding out what needs to be done and then taking the appropriate and also immediate action to get it done without any distractions and interruptions getting in the way.

One crucial element that contributes towards any part of success is a heart filled with determination. Staying determined is not as easy as it sounds and often a lot of sweat and blood are involved. It does sound scary because determination is backed by the ability to cross fire without fear and to be able to go all the way to the end. Along the line, there are several prerequisites that you have to understand before you can get determined in a way.

Determination goes very well together with discipline. Determination is deciding that something is a fact, or that you are firm about your position. When you are determined to achieve something, you will do whatever it takes to achieve that result.

It is a force of your mind that becomes evident, that will not take no for an answer. In your mind and your heart, you have determined that there is an answer or solution and that you will discover it.

When you have determination, you push beyond resistance in your mind, which says you can't do something, and you find a way to do and do it well. With that same determination, you push yourself physically beyond your comfort level, to new heights of success.

You have determined in your mind the end outcome and until you have achieved that, you do not stop. Through sheer determination alone, many people have achieved great results, and you can too.

Determination with discipline, patience, focus, and stamina can propel you to great successes and great rewards.

Determination is the grit that gets you through a journey. It is the force of will to do all the little details just as well as the big ones.

It is moving through and finding a way when there is no way. It is trying everything and then adding new things to get the results that you want. It is tapping into all your known resources, and pushing past your previous limits, to take the lead.

You are constantly focused on how to achieve the results that you have set for yourself. If you don't know how to proceed, determination helps get you through the next phase, through the steps of learning, growing, and building, one step at a time and one process at a time. There is a strong place deep within you that you tap into when you are exhausted, stumped, or at a dead end. It is from this strong place that determination is born. It says, "I will not be defeated. I will get this task done."

It is here that you press on, that you make a decision not to quit. It is because you have decided that what you are trying to achieve is essential, and worthy for you to complete. You have felt in your heart that the outcome will be very good, Or even great.

All dreams require determination to make a reality. Anyone who accomplished something in this life had great determination to do so.

You can accomplish your dreams with determination.

You can accomplish anything that you want.

Be determined in an outcome and slowly but surely, or even quite rapidly you will see your dreams coming closer and finally become a reality. That is the most excellent feeling in the world: when you have achieved something that you have set out to accomplish. No one can take that feeling, or the work that it took to accomplish it, away from you.

Clearly Agreeing to It

When you are required to work over something and stay determined, you have to first agree to bind to it for as long as it takes. For example, if you strive to lose weight, you have to strike an agreement with yourself first to seriously follow through. You would have to agree to yourself to say that you are going to exercise every day or eat less and stick with the plan for as long as it may take. Now, that does not mean you should not change plans because there are always better means towards an objective, and determination is only objective driven, not action driven. That proves determination on winning over something despite complications, temptations, vulnerabilities and even fallback on the resource. By clearly agreeing to the subject requiring a lot of determination, personally, you achieve an inner harmonium which then allows you to keep going and doing the good work.

Foresee-able Distractions

People often let go when something happens in between causing distractions, hesitations or other deterring factors. Take the example of striving to lose weight, if you get pregnant suddenly, you will stop all your weight lose regimes and embark on a complete new set of rules on baby-ing diet. Probably, you will have to put on some weight in order to be able to deliver safely, no choice for you. So, if that happens, you will have to remember this, determination is about going all the way to the end, and once you agree to stay determined, that was when you had agreed to venture on a new part in your life altogether. You wanted to lose weight, you were determined, now you could not, but you can do it after wards. Yes, the key is to stay focused even when things happen in between, do not lose pace or you could be taking that part of yourself for granted. Manage your distractions, complications and all else that comes in between unless you are ready to give up for better or worse.

Knowledge, Rights & Will Power

You can only stay determined when you have enough visibility and knowledge over the matter of concern. For example, it is quite impossible to stay determined if you have absolutely no idea about what you are trying to achieve in the first place. Say lose weight—if you have no understanding about absolute health benefits about weight loss or impact on your image and personality, sooner or later, you will lose interest. When that happens, you do not bother any further because you could not see what is so good about that thing you do. Determination can only happen, if you are truly passionate, have a lot of knowledge, experience and will power which will then guide you through that tedious pathways in the journey. So, be sure to seek knowledge first before you want to tell yourself to stay determined. Again, determination is about creating harmony between yourself and your actions, so strive to be determined over something that is going to be right and constructive in the long run.

Love & Hate

To be determined, you must either love or hate. Love brings passion to your heart over something that provides you with a steady flow of continuous energy. For example, you loved animals and, in order to not see any more getting hurt, you strive to build an animal shelter despite all hardships. Or if you fancy something so much, you would work hard to achieve similar goals between yourself and your ideals, to hate would account for a strong desire to bring about change. And this desire itself is going to lead you towards a lot of determination as well. If you hated animal cruelty, you would also strive to set up an animal protection community for example. So be very sure of what you love or hate, you should love or hate truthfully in order to gain a heart that allows you to stay determined.

When Do We Need Determination?

Every one of us has a goal to achieve, a career to follow and a life to grow. It is a fact that every individual always tries to do his best to attain his goals in life, to be successful his career and to live life to the fullest—However, it's not easy to do it. There are obstacles in life to be eradicated. They are the barriers throughout the journey of achieving these desired goals, these chosen careers and these nurtured lives. They affect too much before we achieve the fruit of success. They make us frown, they make us disappointed, they make us burned out, they make us cry and much worse is, they make us totally hopeless. How do we deal with these dilemmas in life to accomplish our goals? How are we going to reach and hit the target? Perhaps, you have asked your many friends, you have consulted many experts and you have taken many actions to seek advice from the different professionals because you have that burning desire to succeed in life. But, sometimes, we forget that the actions to top out our achievement lie in our very own tenacity. And you would even wonder about it—our very own tenacity? Yes, precisely, it is a character that is often left out in molding our hopes and ambitions, and essentially, in climbing the ladder of success.

There are many definitions of this word. The very short and simple meaning that truly catches everyone's mind is "persistent determination." Another meaning states that "tenacity is having the quality to be determined to achieve a goal. People who are tenacious are typically very stubborn about achieving their goal no matter what their limits or what stands in their way". Whys are they described as very stubborn? Is it because they are difficult to manage? Certainly and not! It is because they have the ideal focus to drive their determination to achieve their objectives. And this ideal focus goes with persistent perseverance that serves a strong and powerful weapon to combat all the negative adversaries in life. It is truly significant to combine focus and perseverance to fulfill and carry out the vision to succeed. Are the adversaries helpful to be more persistent to move on? A person needs to strengthen his mind and direct his will to be what he wants to be, to find what he seeks for and to achieve what he dreams up. The famous Alexander Graham Bell once said "What this power is I cannot say; all I know is that it exists and it becomes available only when a man is in that state of mind in which he knows exactly what he wants and is fully determined not to quit until he finds it." Is this the tenacity that he refers to? Yes, it is. Tenacity exists and is available to function when we want to achieve something. Just like our complete determination will activate to pursue and follow the dreams. This will not stop until we succeed.

It's not easy to possess tenacity in life. Likewise, it's not easy to attain success in life. Determination is there but often misused. We partly say "I have the determination" but it doesn't show. Simply, it is because the essence is not used well according to its desired purpose. The execution is weak. The motivation is lacking. How can you get the success that you want if you are directed to a wrong practice? Yes, there is the tenacity that you want but you're not using it well. Like what Nathaniel Bronner Jr. has uttered, "Success is often not a matter of talent, but a matter of tenacity." When our determination is not persistent, we can't survive until the finish line of our dreams. There would be a particular moment to hang on and specific reason to stop. We are given talents to use and be enhanced as we live along the shadows of our dreams. However, the lack of tenacity leads us to be incomplete. And we ask ourselves, "Where did I go wrong? I did my best, but it wasn't enough. How can I go on to achieve this shattered dreams?"

Now, you tend to go back from the start to visualize and reflect what you've done. Where did your tenacity go? We should not forget the powerful line from a poem of Sri Chinmoy, it is written "No determination of the mind, no transformation of the life." He emphasized that our determination starts from the mind. It explains us to think the ways on how to succeed, on how to transform our life into the realm of accomplishment. How will you transform in order to hit the dimension of success will depend on how you practice your tenacity. How far will your persistent determination go will depend on how you carry out the possibilities and opportunities to succeed in life. Let your firmness and persistence serve as the guiding light to follow the track of success. Let tenacity shines until you touch the rewarding moment of success!

How to Build Self-Determination
 To be determined is to have a mind that is not easily deterred. It means to have a resolve about a particular issue or item as to how one has chosen to go by it.

Self-determination therefore is a way to stay motivated and inspired throughout a particular situation or circumstance or experience without giving up or stepping out of the boat until the target or aim of the process is accomplished or achieved. It is a personal resolve to always be a winner and never a loser. It is a win-win attitude and mind set.

How do you build your self-determination? There are a number of ways but let us start by discussing just one of them.

Focus.
That is one powerful ingredient and tool that can be used to build one's self-determination. It is not that easy to maintain focus on something. Can you imagine how many things have crossed your mind just within the time you started reading this great information about staying self-determined? That is how challenging it can be to maintain focus and keep going without looking back on a mission or target that has already been set.

You just pay close attention to how quickly we all derail from our goals and dreams and targets to the point of finding it so hard to accomplish something or anything whatsoever it is that can be referred to as being worth a while. We all fall into this loophole very easily.

To conquer this daunting challenge and stay focused in life about all that may be our goals and dreams and targets, we need to have sign posts and yard sticks to measure progress in all that we lay our hands to do.

The sign posts and progress measure bars also have to be simple things that break down huge and large tasks into smaller bits so that it is a thing of joy to celebrate every breakthrough point of achievement. This is very important in maintaining focus and it ultimately help to boost our self-determination.

Anyone can talk about how determined they are in the mind until they encounter some distraction they did not plan for and thought will only take a few seconds or minute but end up clearing them off their feet and flooring their entire goal down the gutter.

Maintaining focus is not an easy task we must conclude but it is possible to achieve it when the idea shared here is employed and properly implemented.

Once you use this idea of focusing on small things along the way to great achievements, let us know how well it has helped you to achieve your goal of building your self-determination both for the short and long term.

Do this effective and straightforward exercise. Take one thing on your task list that has been sitting there for a while;

make sure it is something difficult that you have been putting off for some time. It is not that hard, we all have that one thing on our "to do" list that we ignore, put off, or hope it goes away. Now, take this challenge and get it did. Don't procrastinate any longer on this. Close the door of your office and focus on getting that one task done.

When you have determination, you have the ability to get anything done, nothing can stop you. Many of us lack simple determination and we allows outside forces such as the telephone, email, going out for drinks with friends, water cooler chats and any other distractions that you can think of to interfere with us getting our tasks completed.

Getting stuff done

What separates the winners from the losers in business today? Determination! This simple yet tough word is the reason many people struggle in business today, they simply lack the determination to get stuff done. The strugglers work harder at coming up with excuses and by the time they have mastered an excuse, they could have just got the task done.

Now is the time for you to become personally accountable for your results in your life and business and stop blaming others. If you struggle with getting things done, find someone to help you. There are a number of people out there that you can get to help you, employees, mentors, coaches, family, and many more. People are always willing to help, you just need to ask and sometimes invest in their help.

Here are some basic tips to help you with getting stuff done:

Telephone - Put your telephone on "do not disturb" or turn off the cell phone. The phone will ring; let it ring, if it is important they will leave a message. The task at hand is more important that answering the phone. Experts claim that it is takes the average person ten to 15 minutes to get back on track after an interruption.

Close the door - Close the door to your office and do, not accept any interruptions. Have your assistant or receptionist at the office play the role of the gatekeeper and filter any interruptions.

Get out of the office - I personally do all my writing while I am flying, this article is no exception. You don't have to fly somewhere to get stuff done. You can work from home where it is quiet, or a coffee shop (I like this one, observing behaviors of others is very inspirational). Just get out and away so you can focus.

Accountability - Many organizations today lack accountability. There is this fear about holding people accountable in business today. Successful people are accountable to others, business colleagues and also themselves. I recommend investing in a business mentor or a peer group to assist you in becoming accountable.

Delegate - Delegate tasks that someone else can do. This will allow you to focus on the important items. You can delegate all or just parts of the tasks to assist you in reaching your goal of getting stuff done around your business or life. Anything can be delegated when you have the right team around you.

The important message here is to get things done. The longer you put things off, the harder it is to get on track. Determination is the key to filtering out the distractions and focusing on the items that need to get done. Are you determined to get stuff completed and see your business skyrocket?

Lesson

You have it in you, too. Somewhere deep inside, you have pushed through heartache, pain and isolation and achieved a big win!
Remember that drive that got you through, remember that burning need to finish not knowing the outcome.
Your determination will get you to where you want to be.

11

Great People Who Were Once Failures

We all have, at a point or the other in our lives, made such exclamations and these were made at the lowest points of our lives; times when we failed. So, you are not alone in the game.

Myself, your mentor, your role model, the richest men living and the most intellectual men have failed at some point and are probably still failing.

That you failed a course and your mentor failed to win a contract does not make any of the situations a more pronounced failure.

The definition given to failure in our society today has not only influenced our philosophy but has also made the true essence of failure underestimated.

Failure stories seem absolutely 'deadly' to us that we would rather not give a challenge another try or even try at all. This mentality has left so many in a mediocrity zone when in the actual sense they have potentials to do great stuff.

It is only the few that have taken the courage to see the beauty in failure have actually recorded outstanding success stories in history.

Whereas, the timid sees failure as a menace; a monster, when in the real sense, the accurate description of the failure is well encapsulated in this quote by Henry Ford -' Failure is simply the opportunity to begin again, this time more intelligently.'

Over and over, you have read, listened and absorbed success stories in your intellectual archive and despite the fact that every success story has a process of failure in it, your mental system has been reprogrammed in such a way that it filters the process of failure and wants to only see the happy endings of success, and you run with that.

Then, you fail and you suddenly view it as one of the most unfortunate occurrences that can ever happen to you.

You needs to take a look at the stories of successful people initially tagged as failures.

They didn't allow society's definition to disrupt how they can effectively use the wings of failure to get their destination of success. I am certain that a good look at them will help you have a new perspective on failure.

JACK MA

I really love the story of Jack Ma because of his undying spirit in the pursuit of a great life which eventually got him a bigger package.

Jack Ma (original name: Ma Yun) was a normal child just like everyone in his neighbourhood in south-eastern China. He was not a genius neither was he a computer guru.

He was about 31 years of age when he first saw and operated a computer. His parents weren't rich nor influential, he was born to traditional musicians-storytellers who made meagre income and were below the middle-class in their days.

Nothing was spectacular or peculiar about Jack Ma's early life. He was a normal child, teenager and youth who failed his way through. In short, failure and rejections were a key part of Jack Ma's life.

So, how did he become one of the world's successful men?

He simply embraced failure and moved on.

In His Words, Jack Ma Described His Success Story By Stating The Processes Of Failure Involved.

"I failed a key primary school test two times and failed three times in middle schools. For three years, I tried and failed in the university. I also applied for jobs 30 times and got rejected. I even went to KFC when they came to China.

24 people went for the job, 23 were accepted and I was the only one who got rejected. I applied for Harvard ten times and got rejected. I think we have to get used to rejection. The only thing – Never give up."- Jack Ma.

Failed, rejected, failed, failed, rejected – was an integral part of the life of a man who has, in a great way, influenced the economy of China through technology and is the second richest man in China.

So, it is not over because you've had a series of failures, it can only be over if you give up too soon.

MICHAEL JORDAN

You sure know Michael Jordan. Yeah! That great and successful basketball player. Who would dontknow him?

But have you taken the time to go through his profile? How he courageously took steps on the ladder of failure to the arena of success?

The very major encounter that turned his life around was not an easy one. When in high school, sophomore Michael applied for the varsity basketball team at Larry high school with high hopes of getting considered. But his hopes were smashed against the rock of disappointment when the list was pasted, his name wasn't there. Oops!

Rather, his name appeared on the Junior varsity team. That looks quite demeaning.

He felt so bad, he wanted to give up on sport but his mother believed in him and advised him otherwise—This helped Michael to embrace failure and disappointment in order to get better.

He accepted the junior varsity team and gave himself totally to it and here's one of his statements – ' whenever I was working out and I got tired and figured I had to stop, I'd close my eyes and see that list on the locker room without my name on it and that usually got me going again.'

In his words, 'I Went To My Room, Closed The Door And I Cried. For A While, I Couldn't Stop….'

However, the power of imagination kept him on track. He'll rather fear the imagination of not seeing himself in his desired future than give up. Can you see how magical that can be?

So, when Jordan got into the spotlight, he could not but celebrate his failures because he saw them as a propeller of success.

"I've missed more than 9,000 shots in my career. I've lost almost 300 games. 26 times, I've been trusted to take the game-winning shot and I missed. I've failed over and over and over again in life. And that is why I succeed". – Michael Jordan

Without doubts, Jordan was another man who understood and embraced the probability of failing.

He came to the realization that he can only truly succeed when he has failed because this will give him the needed impetus to try again till he succeeds.

Did he enjoy the process? Not!

But he was open-minded enough to pick the required lessons which later paid off.

Today, Michael Jordan is one of the greatest basketball players ever lived with career statistics that include 6,672 rebounds, 5,633 assists, and 32,292 total points. What a feat!

But that was only possible for a man who understood that failure only means you've got to put in more effort next time.

Catch this: When you are tired of going on, stop, breathe, close your eyes and then picture yourself not being able to achieve that thing because you stopped. Let that push you to keep at it.

STEPHEN KING

"We are not interested in science fiction which deals with negative utopias. They do not sell."

This was the reply Stephen got from one of the publishers who checked the manuscript for "Carrie," the book that later brought him to the spotlight and gave him a major reference in his career. The book "Carrie" was actually rejected 30 whooping times!

Stephen initially accepted defeat and felt that his creative writing skills were not good enough. He later took the last courage as a result of the push his wife gave him and that was it! No wonder the book was specially dedicated to his wife, – Tabitha.

Today, Stephen King Remains One Of The Most Successful And Famous Authors, Having Sold Over 350 Million Books.

However, the rejection of Carrie wasn't the only failure Stephen encountered; he has a series of rejections even from his early teenage years, so much that he hung them on the wall with a nail and later had to change the nail to a spike when the weight of the rejection letters could no longer be supported by the nail.

I'm familiar with people hanging their awards and achievement. But someone hanging rejection letters? That's a big one.

SOICHIRO HONDA

Here are another man who had his fight with failure; series of them, but he never gave up because even though the world did not believe in his vision, he knew his vision was achievable and not even his lack of formal education limited him.

Sochirio started out as an apprentice at an automobile shop at the tender as of 15 and he was an intern for six years after which he started his own automotive shop.

At age 31, he started to create piston rings for Toyota even with little means of survival. He gave his all into the invention but in the end, the invention was rejected by Toyota.

Sochirio did not give up; instead, he went to school to gain more knowledge and enlightenment to further develop his initial design.

This did not come to him on a platter of gold as he did his research for two years with some failures in-between.

After his series of trial and failure, he got it right and was able to secure a contract with Toyota. But that was not the end of it.

Life caught up with Sochirio. When the piston ring he made got exploded, he rebuilt it but the company was again affected by an earthquake.

Sochirio's undefeated spirit wouldn't let him give up and this actually brought him his major success. After the earthquake, he started what was different from piston rings and this led to the creation of the Honda automobile.

Today, his company has grown to be an automotive empire competing with Toyota. Indeed, there is no limit for a man with an undying spirit.

ABRAHAM LINCOLN

Abraham Lincoln remains one of the greatest men that made history.

This happened not only because he was the president of America but because he was a leader with a difference.

Lincoln is a man of immense tenacity; he was a friend to failure.

Let me tell you a little about him.

At age 23, Lincoln lost his job and, at the same time, failed in his bid for the state legislature. Three years later, the woman he, so much loved died.

By The Time He Was 29, He had Contested To Be The Speaker In The Illinois House Of Representative And Still Failed.

Lincoln further failed in his bid to become Commissioner of the General Land Office in D.C. at the age of 49. He lost in his quest to become a U.S. Senator.

Despite the series of heart-rending failings Lincoln experienced in his personal, business and political life, he pressed on.

However, with perseverance, persistence, and optimism, at age 52, Lincoln became the president of the United States of America.

He held the highest office in the US because he never gave in to his numerous defeats.

ALBERT EINSTEIN

What comes to your mind when you hear or see the name, Albert Einstein?

Genius!

I can't be wrong. Albert made himself a figure to reckon with in the world of academia. Now, let's be factual, has Albert always had it with brightness? Hell no!

Albert early life was the complete opposite of what he later became.

Young Albert Had A Delay In Speech, And He Couldn't Speak Until The Age Of 4.

He failed the examination for entrance into the Swiss Federal Polytechnic School located in Zurich and struggled all through his university days. In fact, he narrowly escaped dropping out of school.

It was so terrible that his own father never believed he could amount to anything in life till his death.

However, Albert made the best use of his stockpile of failure which made him one of the most brilliant minds ever lived.

OPRAH WINFREY

"Oprah Winfrey" is not only a household name but a global figure. A woman who has earned class for herself through what she does.

Although Oprah's failure aren't very similar to the persons above, one could say that life failed Oprah.

Born to a single teenage mother in Mississippi, Oprah not only tasted abject poverty while growing up. Still, she also experienced series of sexual molestation as a child which led to the birth of her premature baby at age 14: Though, the baby died afterwards.

Oprah did not let her past get the best of her; she simply put the ugly episodes of her past behind her and moved on to pursue her dreams.

She won a beauty pageant at age 17, had her internship in a radio station and got a job immediately after college.

However, all these little successes were short-lived as she was retrenched from her job and was considered unfit for television broadcast.

The Tv Goddess Was Once Considered 'Unfit'! I Guess You Are Also Shocked.

Oprah kept on pushing, disregarding every obstacle and facing her passion squarely; she later got another job where she took over the fledgeling show called AM Chicago because of her distinct personality.

Afterwards, the show became her own very show – Oprah Winfrey's show and the reason behind her popularity and affluence.

ROBERT T. KIYOSAKI

Yeah! Rich dad, poor dad comes to mind whenever we hear the name, Robert Kiyosaki. Have you ever wondered how a man could effectively tackle and compare the mentality of two different dads as regards finances? He sure did not learn that in the classroom.

Life taught him that. Yes! Through a series of failures.

At 30, Kiyosaki started a business that ran into bankruptcy and failed afterward. After three years, he tried another line of business, but history repeated itself and the business failed again.

His two encounters with failure had equipped him with some knowledge, so he set out to start a financial education company at age 38. He later sold the company after nine years so as to begin a career in investing, and writing.

Although fortune did not smile on Kiyosaki immediately, with perseverance and previous experiences, he was able to scale through. At age 50, he wrote the book that earned him international recognition.

HENRY FORD

Ford did not have it all figured out until the age of 28 when he decided to become an engineer for Edison Illuminating Company. During his years of work with this company, he started experimenting with gasoline engines.

The experiment wasn't successful until after five years when he designed and built a self-propelled vehicle and, with this, he was able to earn the support of William H. Murphy (a lumber baron in Detroit) which lead to the founding of Detroit Automobile Company a year later.

Notwithstanding, the company failed after a while due to debt and inefficiencies in the design of the vehicle.

This was a big blow on Ford, yet he did not give up. He searched for further assistance, and he tried again. This also ended in failure.

The last shot Ford gave his venture was all he did to become one of the most successful industrialists ever lived.

Thank God Ford did give up!

MAYA ANGELOU

Her voice brought liberty, hope and happiness to many; a fearless woman she was; a woman who made a worthwhile living out of her past failures and disappointment.

Maya's parents got divorced when she was only three years, which made her father drop her and her only brother (age 4) with their paternal grandparents.

When she was eight years of age, her father returned them to their mother's care. Unfortunately, she was sexually molested severally by her mother's boyfriend.

She took the courage to inform her brother about it, who later told the rest of the family about it. Coincidentally, her abuser was murdered. This incident silenced Maya for 5 years.

Yes! For five whole years, no one heard a word from Maya. She was in great shock!

She later recounted, ' I thought my voice killed him; I killed that man because I told his name. And then I thought I would never speak again because my voice would kill anyone.'

Maya's life had a series of unpalatable events and flaws. As a young adult, she was exposed to sexually-related jobs which included prostitution and night club entertainment. She had her only child at the age of 17.

She also got married twice, and both marriages failed. She had two major depressions in her adult life; the first was during the assassination of Malcolm X whom she worked with to help build a new civil rights organization (the Organization of Afro-American Unity) and the second depression was during the assassination of Martin Luther King Jr., who she worked with.

Maya had her share of failure and life also failed Maya on several occasions, but she was able to pull through.

She built a voice on the foundation of failure that became a solace to many by becoming an incredible civil rights activist who published several autobiographies, essays and books of poetry.

Through her outstanding works, dozens of awards were accredited to her alongside 50 honorary degrees.

CHRIS GARDNER

Are You Embarrassed by Your FAILURE? Read the failure stories of 20 successful people

Ever saw the movie 'The Pursuit of Happiness'?

That film will certainly bring tears to your eyes. The movie is based on the struggles and failures of the man – Chris Gardner before success eventually located him.

Born in 1954, Chris Gardner had a co-seismic childhood. One could say Gardner fought failure even from childhood, no wonder he became an exceptional father.

As a child, he was confronted with poverty, domestic violence, alcoholism, family illiteracy etc., yet he managed to scale through high school and joined the navy.

Afterwards, he got a job as a medical research associate and started a business of medical equipment distribution. He invested a whole lot of money into this business with the hope that the business would succeed.

Alas! The business failed miserably. This left him bankrupt and, to worsen his situation, his wife left him. This failure did not only affect Gardner but also his very tender son.

It would be so terrible to see his son suffer and become incapacitated—gardner fought every single day to get shelter for himself and his son.

They Moved From Place To Place, Sleeping In Numerous Awkward Places Such As Public Toilets And Parks.

Disregarding his failure in relationship and business, Gardner refused to be miserable. He moved on with life courageously and decided to intern with a brokerage firm where he got very little pay.

He knew his passion lay there, so he worked really, really hard, and his hard work paid off as he succeeded ultimately.

Today, Gardner is the CEO of his own brokerage firm-Gardner Rich in Chicago and his net worth is about $60,000,000.

BILL GATES

This is one man that has become so successful as though he never knew failure—but a deep look into his profile reveals otherwise.

Ever before the successful Microsoft started, Bill gates co-founded a company called Traf-O-Data with Paul Allen in the early 1970s which failed.

Paul Allen later recalled about the company: "Despite efforts to sell our wares as far afield as South America, we had virtually no customers.

Traf-O-Data was a good idea with a flawed business model. It hadn't occurred to us to do any market research, and we had no idea how hard it would be to get capital commitments from municipalities.

Between 1974 and 1980, Traf-O-Data totalled net losses of $3,494. We closed shop shortly after that."

Aside from Gate's failure with Traf-O-Data, He also made some terrible mistakes even as a CEO of Microsoft which cost the company terribly.

Nevertheless, the truth remains that the flunk of Bill's first company, Traf-O-Data, played a major part in the success of Microsoft because Bill learnt greatly from it.

BEN CARSON

Benjamin Carson was born on September 18, 1951, in Detroit, Michigan, to Robert and Sonya Carson. He began his education in Detroit Public Schools where he was an average student.

When Carson was eight, his parents got separated and he moved with his mother.

Due to the financial limitation of his mother, Carson and his brother had to attend a two-classroom school at the Berea Seventh-day Adventist church where two teachers taught eight grades, and the vast majority of time was spent singing songs and playing games.

When they returned to Detroit public schools, Carson and his brother's academic performance lagged far behind their new classmates, having essentially lost a year of school by attending the small Seventh-day Adventist parochial school in Boston. He consecutively took the least grade in school.

His Transition

His transition began when their mother limited their time watching television and required them to read and write book reports on two library books per week. With this measure, he eventually improved greatly in his Academics and topped the class.

He is a graduate of Yale University and the University Of Michigan Medical School. Carson became the Director of Pediatric Neurosurgery at Johns Hopkins Hospital in Maryland from 1984 until he retired in 2013.

He achieved numerous feats in the medical world like performing the only successful separation of conjoined twins joined at the back of the head; separation of type-2 vertical craniopagus twins—he developed new techniques for controlling seizures and methods for detecting brain tumors.

Currently, he is serving as the 17th United States Secretary of Housing and Urban Development since 2017, under Donald Trump's Administration.

He is a recipient of the Presidential Medal of Freedom, the highest civilian award in the United States.

NELSON MANDELA

Nelson Mandela was born on 18th July 1918 to the Thembu royal family in Mvezo, British South Africa and died on the 5th of December 2013.

He studied law at the University of Fort Hare and the University of Witwatersrand and then worked as a lawyer in Johannesburg.

In South Africa, he fought dearly against the apartheid system in the South. He was arrested and imprisoned in 1962 due to his struggle against the white's one-government system.

Subsequently, he was sentenced to life imprisonment for conspiring to overthrow the state following the Rivonia Trial.

Mandela served 27 years in prison and got released amidst growing domestic and international pressure in 1990. Due to his leadership demeanour, he was elected as the president of South Africa in 1994.

While serving as the president, he worked toward unity between the countries' racial groups and established a commission to investigate past human rights.

Unlike most politicians, Mandela declined a second presidential term and was succeeded by his deputy in 1999. He later became an elder statesman who focused on combating poverty and HIV/AIDS through the charitable Nelson Mandela Foundation.

Mandela's activism is internationally recognized and held in deep respect within South Africa. He is often regarded as the father of the Nation and an icon of democracy and social justice. A 1993 winner of the Nobel Peace Prize.

MICHAEL FARADAY

Michael Faraday was born on the 22nd of September 1791 and died on the 25th of August 1867.

Faraday was one of four children who worked hard to get enough to eat since their father was a blacksmith and was often ill and incapable of working steadily.

He Got Only The Rudiments Of Education – To Read And Write – From A Church Sunday School.

At an early age, he began to earn money by delivering newspapers for a book dealer and bookbinder and became his apprentice at the age of 14.

Unlike the other apprentices, Faraday took the opportunity to read some of the books brought in for rebinding and he spent the next seven years educating himself by reading books on a wide range of scientific subjects.

In 1812, Faraday attended four lectures given by the chemist Humphry Davy at the Royal Institution.

Faraday subsequently wrote to Davy asking for a job as his assistant. Davy turned him down but, in 1813, appointed him as a chemical assistant at the Royal Institution, helping with experiments for Davy and other scientists.

In 1821, he published his work on electromagnetic rotation (the principle behind the electric motor). After that, Faraday discovered electromagnetic induction, the principle behind the electric transformer and generator.

He contributed greatly to the study of electromagnetism and electrochemistry. His main discoveries include the principles underlying electromagnetic induction, diamagnetism and electrolysis.

His inventions were of utmost benefit to mankind. He invented electricity even without proper education.

THOMAS EDISON

One could say Thomas Edison was the most optimistic man ever lived. How could one does not give up after recording 10,000 failed attempts on a particular experiment?

Born on the 11th of February, 1847, Edison was the seventh and last child – the fourth surviving – of Samuel Edison, Jr., and Nancy Elliot Edison.

At an early age, he developed hearing problems, which have been variously attributed but were most likely due to a familial tendency to mastoiditis.

Edison's deafness strongly influenced his behavior and career, providing the motivation for many of his inventions. Edison only attended school for a few months and was instead taught by his mother.

He Failed 10,000 Times To Invent A Commercially Viable Electric Light Bulb, But He Didn't Give Up.

When asked by a newspaper reporter if he felt like a failure and would like to give up, Edison simply stated "Why would I feel like a failure? And why would I ever give up? I now know definitely over 9,000 ways an electric light bulb will not work. Success is almost in my grasp."

This is the same person whose teachers said he was "too stupid to learn anything," and fired from his first two employment positions for not being productive enough.

However, Edison, through his failures, is also the greatest innovator of all time with 1,093 US patents to his name, along with several others in the UK, and Canada.

This is a man who refused to ever give up no matter what.

He attributed his success to his mother, who pulled him out of school and began to teach him herself. Aren't these kinds of mothers awesome?

COLONEL HARLAND SANDERS

Oh! The uniqueness of KFC chicken! But have you ever taken time to read the profile of the man behind the KFC chicken recipe?

Let me give you a quick one, Failure to secure a good job brought about the world's fast food chicken chain. That's amazing, ain't it?

Have you ever heard about the popular saying that goes, 'when life throws a lemon at you, make lemonade out of it'? Yeah! Sanders made very good use of the saying because he made a very unique lemonade.

Having faced rejection and disappointment on several occasions as regards securing a good job and a good life, Sanders did not see himself as one of the failure stories in life, rather he looked inward and saw what he could give to the world if the world was not ready to offer him anything good.

And that's it! He gave us an ever delicious chicken.

Sanders did not make it big immediately after KFC but yet he stayed strong and here is one of his sayings, "I made a resolve then that I was going to amount to something if I could.

And no hours, nor amount of labour, nor the amount of money would deter me from giving the best that there was in me."

ELIZABETH ARDEN

A very successful business mogul born in 1878 also had her share of failures before eventually creating a novel beauty empire by 1929 that included 150 salons throughout the United States and Europe, and eventually selling over 1000 products across 22 separate countries.

Today, the company – Elizabeth Arden, Inc. makes over $1 billion in annual sales, making it one of the most successful beauty businesses.

Nevertheless, there was a period in Arden's life when she failed woefully in business. Yet, she picked up the pieces that failure made of her business and built a magnificent success for herself.

I will conclude with the famous saying that goes, 'it is not over until it is over.' Inasmuch as you are still breathing, there is no failure or circumstances you are facing right now or that you will face that is insurmountable.

Lessons

The definition given to failure in our society today has not only influenced our philosophy but has also made the true essence of failure underestimated.

If you have failed at anything in life, you are able to achieve massive success. This may sound like a strange statement but it is very true. Some of the biggest success stories you will ever hear come from failures.

12

The Lessons I Learned
from Failure

In life, it's necessary to fail. Failure is a steppingstone. In fact, there are five very powerful life lessons that failure helps to teach and instill in us. If you've recently failed at something in a major way, and you're going through a difficult time right now, keep this important lessons in mind.

Experience
The first important lesson gained from failure is experience.

What happens when we fail? When we go through something and can walk away with firsthand experience, it helps us to develop a deeper understanding for life.

The experience of failing at something is genuinely invaluable. It completely alters our frame-of-mind through the induction of pain. It makes us reflect on the real nature of things and their importance in our lives, transforming and improving our future-selves.

I once created a monthly tourism journal called Bad Füssing aktuell in Bad Füssing/Germany in partnership with the local tourism office. Bad Füssing is by far the most visited thermal spa in Europe and it started successfully. One day, a young man came in my office and offered to sell his very mediocre Kitzbühel Magazine. I liked the brand name "trendguide", the size of the journal but not the content. I offered him a large sum and he was happy so much so that he even brought his computer for free and he left to look for a future in Australia.

I remodeled the magazine and got my first big clients by phone. We released two trendguide magazines a year and enjoyed the growing business.

This business came after I sold my agency. I wanted to create a business that would grow steadily without my involvement. I created a partner and license model and the dream was to have 100 trendguides in different locations.

Business picked up and we later had an office in Munich; we also had partners all over from Cannes to Italy; in Germany, too. I created the first multimedia content and an App. We also did all bookings and the whole administration online, the first in our business.

The launch of the company was very intense and time consuming and I had to invest a lot of effort and money in the business.

After some time, my partners learned the business and were becoming illoyal. They quit and founded their own magazines.

They told the clients strange stories to poach them, and operated under false flag.

It was a horrible experience for me, betrayals from trusted people in my late years. I started losing money.

I didn't want to involve lawyers and start any legal battles because it was not worth it.

A couple of years later, I decided to partner with a couple I knew for years and they had been eager to partner up. I loved the idea.

I left town for a while and left the partners to run the business. When I returned, everything was upside down. They had no clue. We had to split up and I paid them back and again I was in charge.

But the publishing business was hard, there were only very few reliable people, and there were a lot of hypocrites.

After a couple of years, I decided to pull back all investments in-app, and multi media content just stopped.

Slowly, the business recovered till the pandemic took its toll.

As of the time I'm writing this, the business has started recovering from damage the pandemic did on us.

Knowledge
Failure brings with it important firsthand knowledge. That knowledge can be harnessed in the future to overcome that

very failure that inflicted so much pain in the first place. Nothing can replace the knowledge gained from failure.

I constructed a big house with holiday apartments and started to rent out using AIRBNB and other providers.

I had much fun, international visitors, and good money, but I started to realize that I was the slave of my property. No, thank you – I want to be free…

We hired a host company that is now running the business.

When Thomas Edison famously failed nearly 10,000 times to create a commercially viable electric lightbulb, with each failure, he gained the knowledge of just one more avenue that work. It was the accumulated knowledge developed from nearly 10,000 failed attempts that ultimately led to his success.

Resilience

Failing in life helps to build resilience. The more we fail, the more resilient we become.

In order to achieve great success, we must know resilience. Because, if we think that we're going to succeed on the first try, or even the first few tries, then we're sure to set ourselves up for a far more painful failure.

The characteristic of resilience can help us in so many ways in life. Resilience helps to breed success by setting the game up to win. Gone are the lofty expectations that things will happen overnight, and in comes the expectations that true success will take an enormous amount of work and effort.

Growth

When we fail, we grow and mature as human beings. We reach deeper meanings and understandings about our lives and why we're doing the things that we're doing. This helps us to reflect and take things into perspective, developing meaning from painful situations.

Life is designed for us to grow and improve. From the very genetic fibers that make us into who, we are as individual persons, into the fabric of society on a global scale, growth is a fundamental part of us. Without growth, we couldn't improve life on every front.

Value

One of the biggest lessons that we can learn from life's failures is the necessity to create and spread an exceedingly high amount of value. In fact, value lies at the heart of success and a lack of value is a fundamental pillar to failure.

In thinking about your past failures, think about how much value you brought to the table. Could you have offered more value? Would that have prevented failure? When you learn to create immense value, and do so consistently, you will eventually succeed.

My story eventually led to my brand new start up brainchild, MY- **Mindguide.** I used the COVID lockdown period to study Hypnotherapy, Meditation Yoga. So I'm now a certified Hypno

MasterCoach, Meditation teacher, Yoga teacher and member in the leading Guilds.

My first thought was that the whole mindfulness business lacked marketing and advertising skills and I knew I could deliver successfully in that area.

I put together a presentation about the founding of my-mindgude Club concept to bring a substantial number of Mindfulness professionals in the electronic age.

CONCLUSION

I love hearing stories about people who have overcome huge defeats and struggles to achieve great success in their lives. It's always made me believe I can do the same. I'm a big fan of magazines about entrepreneurs for this reason. You'll find a multitude of business owners who tell stories of how they struggled through bankruptcy, lack of clients, and dozens of people telling them no. But, today, they are multi-million dollar companies with devoted customers. I can't get enough of these stories because it keeps me inspired to continue reaching for higher goals. My failures will eventually give me an inspiring story to tell.

Other times, I hear a story of someone who is currently going through the exact same failure I am. It's great to know that there's someone out there who is going through the same struggles you are. Of course, I'm not happy someone else struggling, but it's nice reminder that you're not the only one who's failed in life. One of the cool things about people who have gone through the same things is that a support system comes into place, which serves to help everyone involved. This is how I've made many new friendships and contacts with people who've shared my personal and career failures.

One thing I've learned is that people respond to honesty. They appreciate when someone is being genuine about themselves, and has the courage to share something that others would be ashamed or humiliated to reveal publicly. There's certainly nothing more honest than admitting how you've failed.

Celebrate Your Failure

Admitting my past failures, and the ones I'll make in the future has set me free. I really do feel as if I have permission to go the distance with my ideas and the things I want in life. Sharing your struggles means you're taking ownership of your failures, and that's one step closer to success. And who knows, your failure may just be an inspiration for someone else.

Be proud and celebrate failure!

If you enjoyed this title and would like to read about other topics that have changed my life, please check out my new books on Amazon or my website:

www.my-mindguide.com

Also, let's stay connected on social media. Please drop a line on Facebook or Instagram, and stay tuned for updates! You're welcome to share your thoughts with me directly as well: gassner@my-mindguide.com. In return, I'll send you a gorgeous infographic that you can cut out and frame.

Also, please leave a review on Amazon, as this will help me to reach an even broader audience. Thank you so much for your time, insight, and undying hunger for knowledge!

I want to say thank you to all of my colleagues, clients, friends, and family members, who have all contributed to what I am now.

I also want to say thank you to Gabriel Palacios, the king of hypnotherapy and a Swiss bestseller author who taught this old fox new tricks, letting me deep-dive into the mystery of hypnotherapy. I learned so much along the journey that I'm now a certified master-hypnosis coach and conversation coach myself!

Furthermore, I want to say thank you to the fantastic teachers of SAMYANA/Bali who trained me to become a certified yoga and meditation teacher.

Last but not least, I give a special thanks to my master-teacher Eckhard Wunderle, who's close to a saint to me. He introduced me to the world of meditation and let me discover all the wonders it has to offer. I could not be more proud about having received my certification as a meditation teacher from directly from him at the Institut für Spirituelle Psychologie.

Peace, love, and happiness to all of you—till next time!

Authors portrait

Kurt Friedrich Gassner has worn many hats throughout his lifetime, including but not limited to serial entrepreneur, Creative Director, Meditation Teacher, Licensed Hypnotherapist, and more recently, self-improvement author. Leveraging his treasure trove of experiences and in-depth knowledge of psychology, he provides his readers with the tools they need to unlock their infinite potential.

As a prolific self-help writer, Kurt has authored the following books: *The Art of Forgiveness, Lie or Die, Soul-Match, Can You Inherit a Poisoned Mind?* and *The Power of Poverty*. He also authored a best-selling children's book in German-speaking countries and has over 20 books underway.

When it comes to enduring success, Kurt understands that financial prosperity isn't the only aspect one should strive for. He may be a self-made millionaire, but what really transformed his life is mastering his unconscious mind. Perseverance, personal power, self-awareness, and learning from past mistakes have all been key ingredients to bringing his dreams to fruition—and he strives to impart that wisdom onto others through his writing.

During his spare time, Kurt Friedrich Gassner is either traveling across the globe, golfing, biking in the Alps, hiking, or spending quality time with his loved ones. For the last 37 years, he has been happily married and he is the father of two successful children. Presently, he resides in both Munich, Germany, and Kirchberg, Austria.

OTHER BOOKS BY THE AUTHOR

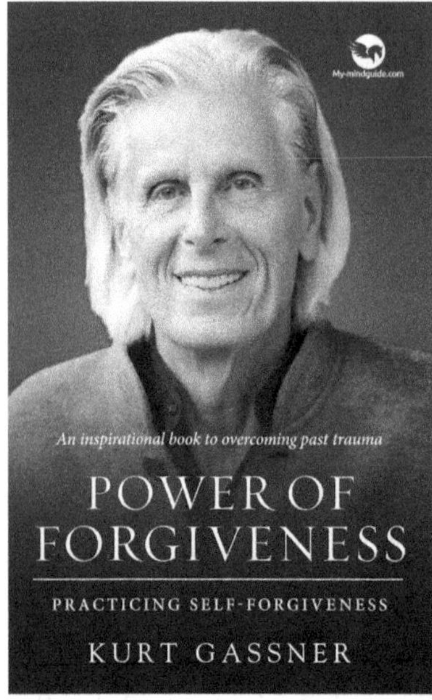

OTHER BOOKS BY THE AUTHOR

My-mindguide.com
GROW
WITH YOUR
FAILURES
GROW THROUGH YOUR FAILURES
KURT GASSNER

My-mindguide.com
WACHSE
MIT DEINEN
MISSERFOLGEN
WACHSE DURCH DEINE MISSERFOLGE
KURT GASSNER

My-mindguide.com
Lass
Los!
Verändere dein Unter- Bewusstsein, befreie dich
von materieller Abhängigkeit & wahre Lebensgeschichten
KURT GASSNER

My-mindguide.com
Let
Go
Rewire your subconscious mind with hypnosis
& cure material addiction – Real Life Stories
KURT GASSNER

OTHER BOOKS BY THE AUTHOR

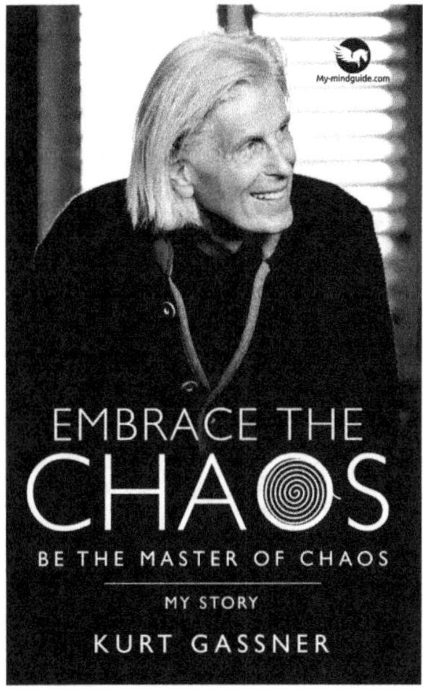

OTHER BOOKS BY THE AUTHOR

OTHER BOOKS BY THE AUTHOR

BORN
in the
COLD
Liebe und Aufmerksamkeit in der Wachstumsphase eines Kindes
KURT GASSNER

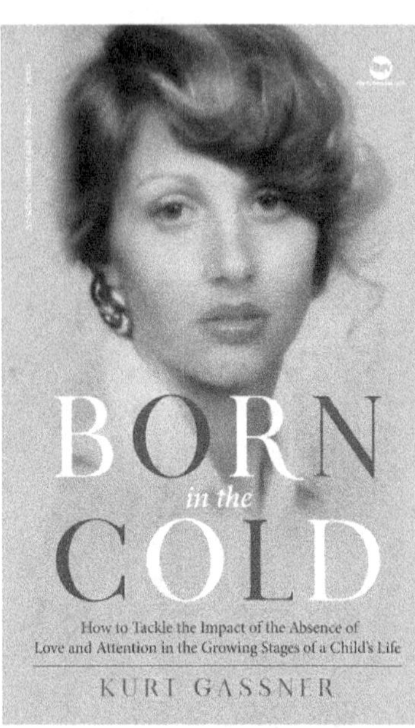
BORN
in the
COLD
How to Tackle the Impact of the Absence of
Love and Attention in the Growing Stages of a Child's Life
KURT GASSNER

SOPHIAS WUNDERWELT
Erzählungen & Kitzbühel in den Kitzbüheler
Alpen in Tirol Österreich
10 ERZÄHLUNGEN
KURT GASSNER

SOPHIA'S WONDERWORLD
of Kitzbühel-Kitzbühel in the Austrian Alps
10 TALES
KURT GASSNER

BESTSELLING AUTHOR OF
The Art Of
FORGIVNESS
AMAZON
#1
BESTSELLER
My-mindguide.com
A practical guide for
self healing and
overcome past traumas
The Art Of
FORGIVNESS
KURT GASSNER
My-mindguide.com
A practical guide for
self healing and
overcome past traumas
The Art Of
FORGIVNESS
KURT GASSNER

www.ingramcontent.com/pod-product-compliance
Lightning Source LLC
LaVergne TN
LVHW050626200726
843506LV00010B/1136